55

40¢

**GOING
INTO
POLITICS**

*a guide
for
citizens*

This book was written by Mr. Merriam and Mrs. Goetz under a grant from The Maurice and Laura Falk Foundation of Pittsburgh. However, the foundation is not the author, proprietor, or publisher of the book and is not to be understood, by virtue of its grant, as endorsing any statement made or view expressed therein.

GOING
INTO
POLITICS

a guide for citizens

BY **ROBERT E. MERRIAM**

AND **RACHEL M. GOETZ**

HARPER
& BROTHERS
*New
York*

CONTENTS

Preface: TWO POLITICAL TESTAMENTS   vii

Introduction: YOU AND DEMOCRACY   1

PART I. *POLITICS IN ACTION: FIRST-HAND ACCOUNT*

One. INSIDE AN ELECTION:

CITIZEN-POLITICIANS AT WORK   9

PART II. *CITIZENS IN POLITICS*

Two. BEGINNER'S GUIDE TO PRACTICAL POLITICS   53

Three. CITIZEN ACTION AND

THE TWO-PARTY SYSTEM   73

Four. THE CITIZEN AND POLITICAL DECISIONS—

LEADERS AND ISSUES   109

v

vi   *Contents*   .

Five. A CITIZEN'S EYE-VIEW OF THE BALLOT BOX   133

Six. PROFESSIONALISM AND POLITICS   151

PART III. *THE ART OF THE POSSIBLE*

Seven. POLITICAL ACTION:
THE ART OF THE POSSIBLE   185

Index   212

Two Political Testaments

This book is a political duet. One of the authors is a Republican, the other is a Democrat. One is a professional politician, the other kept her amateur standing until recently. The professional trained for a career in public administration and has worked for such public agencies as the National Housing Agency and the United States Bureau of the Budget. He has twice run successfully for the office of alderman, and once unsuccessfully for mayor of Chicago. The amateur participated as a volunteer in four aldermanic, one mayoral, two senatorial, one gubernatorial, one presidential, and assorted minor campaigns. She turned semi-pro in the 1956 presidential election, writing with the editorial and research division of the Stevenson campaign staff. She also worked with the Merriams, father and son, on their college text, *The American Government: Democracy in Action*. She conducted a pilot study of audio-visual communication in public service training and civic education for Public Administration Clearing House.

Both of us value our personal independence in politics. We have worked with groups like the Independent Voters of Illinois, the League of Women Voters, and in a wide variety of other civic ventures. Neither enjoys being "beholden," yet we are both deeply committed to the American two-party system.

We believe that it plays an important and unique role in the forward press of democracy and we are convinced that responsible parties are essential to the operation of American governmental institutions.

We believe therefore that the role of the political independent, however important in any particular set of circumstances, must for the long pull take second place to dedicated work within the parties themselves. Thus for all of our maverick tendencies we are both enthusiastic and committed party members—on different sides of the political fence.

We are most grateful to The Maurice and Laura Falk Foundation for this opportunity to gather together these varied strands. We have tried to use our experiences as the anvil against which to shape the links in our story of citizens and their government. We have found that our differences are small in comparison with our areas of agreement. Each has felt privileged to exercise an "item veto" (except in Chapter One), but almost always simple rephrasing has melted away issues. Naturally our experiences and the foci of our interests are different, and our emphases and appraisals of what is desirable and practical reflect these differences.

But we both deeply believe in *the purpose of this book, which is to introduce citizen-politicians to the pleasures and pains of civic action.* We have found that being members of different parties has been no bar to this collaborative effort. With its completion we find ourselves able, in good conscience, to retire to our respective political camps. We can disagree on the issue of personal allegiance to the parties of our choice yet agree completely on the importance of having a party of choice. And we believe that this book will be of more use to other citizen-politicians for the very fact of our own political differences.

ROBERT E. MERRIAM

RACHEL M. GOETZ

INTRODUCTION

You and Democracy

This is a book about you and your handiwork. You, collectively, have created this democracy. You select its leaders. You give it direction. You run it; you can ruin it. It can be corrupted through selfishness and destroyed by neglect. If your vigilance falters, grasping hands will be only too glad to take over. *Democracy means you.* The Greeks supplied the word for it: *demos,* the people, and Lincoln crystallized its meaning for all of us: "Government of the people, by the people, for the people." That is the way we want it; that is the way it can be. But it is far from sure that this is the way it *will* be. The decision is up to you.

Democracy has to be worked at. This is a difficult and demanding business in a world that is full of a number of things, all changing. The voice of the people must speak through tens of millions of lips. The purposes of the people must be translated into meaningful and related actions. *It is the task of politics to harmonize the voices of democracy into a full-throated chorus which will provide the guidance for fruitful action.*

This book takes you on a conducted tour through the mazes of political action. Its purpose is to help you find your niche in the most rewarding, most illusive, most demanding business in the world: the business of being an American citizen. Its

1

subject is bigger than the great American game of politics, though there are few more exciting games. At stake is your future, the future of the United States, indeed the future of civilization.

Every one of us wants things which only government— democratic government—can give us. Even the sturdiest individualist expects government to see that the mails get through. We demand as a right good schools, regular garbage collection, efficient fire departments, and a vigilant police force. In these threatening times we count on our government to maintain a defense establishment second to none, complete—if it must be—with H bombs. Even the Russians want these things. But we in this country demand more. We expect our government to keep freedom's shield bright. We see freedom large: as opportunity and choice, as freedom of economic opportunity and freedom of person, of conscience, and of speech. We count on our government to help us widen steadily the horizons of personal opportunity. We expect it to make good our promises to each other, promises of liberty and justice for all. But most of all *we expect government to keep its place,* to remain in the background, the instrument, the servant of all the people.

Not all of these aspirations are new. Perhaps all that is truly new about them is the intensity of our determination to use government and not let it use us. We have come to this position honestly, along a well-marked course.

It should not be necessary to argue the merits of democracy; the idea of people-centered governments has universal appeal. Even the Soviets make political hay by calling their system "the people's democracy." But at home and abroad, behind the propaganda use of the magic word "democracy" there lurk the siren voices of collectivism; they purr that they can do better for you than you can do for yourself. Democracy is on trial in a world that at least gives it lip service.

We for whom democracy is the cornerstone of our lives can

defend it only through action. We have to be *practicing* citizens; we also have to be *knowledgeable* citizens. Political ignorance in a democracy can be only slightly less damaging than political chicanery. We have to know how and where to make the weight of each one of us felt. Citizenship is not something to be put on and taken off like a hat; it cannot even be treated as a hobby; it is the *business* of everybody. Its rewards are not often measured in dollars; but they profoundly affect the American standard of living and every other value we hold dear.

Political democracy is woven into the fabric of the American way of life; *yet in 1956 some 40 million adult citizens didn't even go to the polls to vote for a President.* The brutal fact is that we still take this wonderful human invention—the free election—for granted. We treat it negligently. We are loud in our protests when it does not work to suit us, louder still when someone tries to snatch it from our grasp. Such political ambivalence is a serious and wasting disease. It drains away much needed national strength; it seriously handicaps the pursuit of the American dream. And it does not make good sense.

Americans are enormously proud of their democratic government and their traditions of freedom, and they will not knowingly settle for any other. Yet they lie down on the job of making it run. This is largely unintentional; we simply do not realize that each of us, individually, must provide its motive power and its direction. Incidentally, of course—it is to our personal advantage to see to it that the government's actions suit us personally. If things go awry, we are quick to blame the wickedness of the other fellow, but the fact is that we are collectively responsible if the rascals take over.

The key to much of our civic lassitude lies in the fact that "we know not what we do." The defenses of this ignorance are high but not insurmountable. They cannot be lightly hurdled once and for all, for the business of democratic participation in present-day government is too complicated to be digested whole.

In the belief that the best attack lies along the path of self-interest, this guidebook to politics is designed as a citizen's-eye view. It attempts to answer the question: "What does an ordinary, garden-variety American want and need to know about the way in which his political world works?" The authors have started on the familiar ground of personal experience and let the generalizations grow from there. Since one of us was the losing candidate in the 1955 campaign for mayor of Chicago, and the other was attached to the staff of a defeated presidential candidate, this equips us to speak personally, and with feeling, on the pains of politics, if not its pleasures! We hasten to add that our candidate had won twice in aldermanic elections and our amateur had worked for a number of successful contenders.

Every campaign is educational to both loser and winner; both are essential to the contest, and around their activities and their political fortunes swirl all the issues, forces, personalities, and parties of the campaign. Such elections lie at the heart of democratic government. They provide key opportunities to citizens to pick and choose, to register significant choices on men and issues. Every election settles some issues—and always leaves more unsettled—but at the least it determines who shall hold the contested office. There is firm logic, therefore, in beginning a book on citizen participation in government, as this one begins, with an election.

But in democracy, elections are only the emergent one-tenth of the political iceberg. Large, powerful, threatening realities lie beneath the surface. A play-by-play account of an actual and heated election—though guaranteed to be good reading—will not suffice to orient citizens as to their total roles in democracy. Therefore, Chapters Two through Six dissect and apply the lessons of the Chapter One case study to you, your community, and your political life. Chapter Two is a beginner's guide designed to help citizen-politicians penetrate and move around inside a political party. Channels for citizen action, especially political parties, are explored in Chapter Three; and Chapter Four puts the selection process under the citizens' microscope. Chapter Five takes a hard look at the ballot box itself. Chapter Six surveys the business of government and politics, topside, from the viewpoint of increasingly important professionalism. Chapter Seven explores still larger reaches of citizen participation and political action and tries to tie down the fascinations, frustrations, and the mechanisms of "Politics: the Art of the Possible."

If you stay with this book to the end you may understand why a defeated candidate still thinks that the game is worth more than the contemplation; and why both authors believe that informed and dedicated citizens working through the parties of their choice can hold to the high purpose of government of the people, by the people, and for the people.

PART I

Politics in Action: A First-Hand Account

CHAPTER ONE

Inside an Election: Citizen-Politicians at Work

NOTE: This is a candidate's eye-view of the election
for mayor of Chicago in April 1955. The story,
presented in the first person, was written entirely
by Robert E. Merriam.

A CONTAGIOUS DISEASE?

Some people say that politics is a contagious disease. I come
from a family which might be cited as evidence in support of
that suspicion. Ours had mixed political views. My mother's
father was a Democratic postmaster named Doyle in a small
upstate New York village. My father's father was the Republican postmaster of a rural Iowa town. My father's cousin
migrated from the same town to California and became the
Republican governor of that state. My mother's sister was until
she recently retired the Democratic-appointed postmistress in
a New York town near her first home.

And the chain has remained unbroken. My father, Charles
E. Merriam, was three times alderman in the City of Chicago
(1909–11, 1913–15, and 1915–17), twice a candidate for mayor
of that city (1911 and 1919), and once recipient of a vote as
vice-presidential candidate (1912, Bull Moose Convention).

9

Not to be outdone by this tradition (although "retired" now at thirty-eight), I have been alderman in Chicago for two terms (1947–51 and 1951–55) and candidate for mayor once (1955). In fact, this father-and son team holds the dubious honor of being the negative counterpart of Chicago's famous Harrison family—Carter Harrison, father and son—who were between them ten times mayor of Chicago. The Merriams, father and son, have been three times defeated candidates for the office.

The case of the two Merriams grows even more strange when one realizes that the 1911 Republican mayoralty nominee and the 1955 Republican mayoralty nominee not only had the same name but were (at the time they ran) identical in age, ran for mayor while alderman, had investigated municipal waste and inefficiency, led crime investigations, and had been crusaders for governmental reform in Chicago. So much for this unpardonable recall. This is not a family history, but rather a personal account of the happenings leading up to election night, April 5, 1955.

It All Began . . .

Maybe it began with that family disease. Perhaps it was that night in 1931 when I accompanied my father to a gigantic political rally near the steel mills to hear one of the greatest of the political spellbinders—Senator J. Hamilton Lewis. It could have started in 1936 when I helped in the campaign of a friend running for the state legislature; or in 1938 when I worked in a precinct for another friend running for Congress (and counted the ballots for a confused election board); or in 1939 when I worked in an aldermanic contest for another friend; or in 1940 when I stumped the street corners in a presidential campaign. Or it could have been during my long wartime service when I had lots of time to think.

Officially, it began on February 22, 1947, when I won a bitterly fought contest to be alderman of the Fifth Ward, City of Chicago. In a real sense this was a fluke. Despite the family political traditions, I had been educated and trained for a full-time career in government service—a civil servant or, more likely, a professional city manager. My work before and after the war was all pointed in this direction. But a bitter fight developed in the Democratic Party in our ward between the alderman and the committeeman (the elected party leader in the ward). As a by-product of this conflict, I was given the support as an independent candidate for alderman that helped me to defeat the incumbent.

In those days Chicago was the last of the patronage-machine-dominated cities, a remnant from the era of Bosses Platt and Pendergast and the old Tammany Hall. Dominated since the first election of Franklin Roosevelt in 1932 by a Democratic machine built around Mayors Cermak and Kelly, Chicago unfortunately had developed a worldwide reputation as the crime and corruption capital of the nation. But in the mid-1940's the machine began playing politics with the school system, and in 1946 citizen unrest boiled over (spurred by a threat from the North Central Education Association that it would refuse accreditation to the Chicago schools). This threat made even traditionally apathetic Chicagoans angry, led to reform in the school board (appointed by the mayor), and eventually to the "dumping" of Mayor Kelly by his own machine, and nomination of a businessman-civic leader as the Democratic candidate for mayor in 1947. This man, Martin Kennelly, was elected over his Republican ward committeeman opponent in one of the largest turnouts at any municipal election in Chicago's history.

That April night of inauguration in 1947 appeared to be the dawning of a new era in Chicago's stormy political history. Although the youngest member of the City Council, I was not the only newcomer. Swept into office in the reform wave were other young aldermen. Several like myself were war veterans, and although the oldtimers of the Democratic organization were in solid majority, we newcomers looked with great hope to Mayor Kennelly for support. Chicago's City Council is nonpartisan in name, but not in spirit. Although most of the new, younger aldermen were Republicans and although I had been elected mostly with Democratic and independent support, we early found many things in common and gradually shaped together a group which eventually was labeled the "economy bloc" (because of our fights for the elimination of waste in city spending).

Mayor Kennelly took some important steps to improve the city's government: The reform in the school system was continued and a new nonpolitical superintendent was brought to Chicago to operate the schools; civil service administration was revitalized; a new central purchasing system was installed with a nonpolitical head who substituted business practices for the political favoritism of the past; a large-scale program of housing and slum clearance was launched, starting a long-overdue rebuilding of the inner parts of the city; garbage collection was restored to a reasonable basis (from once every two weeks irregularly to once a week regularly); long-postponed public improvements and equipment replacement were started; and a scandalous situation in the Municipal Tuberculosis Sanitarium was stopped. In all of these things, I was one of the enthusiastic supporters and aides of the mayor, usually in opposition to the grumbling of rebellious Democratic machine aldermen who saw some of their perquisites being eaten away.

But there were some danger signs. Many of the Kelly appointees remained in command of the various city departments. In other areas, particularly city finances, the mayor appeared reluctant to assume aggressive leadership. Evidence presented later to our Crime Committee indicated that centralized corruption had simply become decentralized; in the organized-crime field the "fix," where it was made, was now at the district level rather than city-wide; in purchasing, several specific cases indicated that strange things sometimes took place in City Council rather than with departmental purchase; it was believed by many that the payment of per-quisites for legitimate favors—driveway permits, zoning varia-tions, and the like—continued unabated and perhaps on a larger scale in the City Council. Gradually it was commonly accepted that the machine aldermen had become the bosses in too many areas of municipal administration.

Despite the rumblings, in 1951 Mayor Kennelly was re-elected easily, still with widespread civic and newspaper support, though with less enthusiasm than in 1947. And I was reelected almost without opposition in that same year. How-ever, the Democratic organization of our ward was clearly unhappy that I was not controllable, and I subsequently dis-covered that they would have opposed me in 1951 had it not been for a debacle in November of 1950 when the city and county Democratic leaders had tried, and disastrously failed, to elect "the world's richest policeman" (as the Kefauver Com-mittee described the gentleman) to the office of sheriff of Cook County.

Things came to a head in December of 1951 when the 1952 city budget was under consideration. Our economy bloc proposed cuts in the budget totaling $6 million in items which we knew or suspected to be heavily padded with waste and/or political workers.

One item in particular demonstrated the machine's attitude. It was an item of $90,000 for chauffeurs for water-meter readers. When asked why they needed chauffeurs for the meter readers, the bureau head said that the chauffeurs lifted the manhole covers on industrial meters so that the reader could go into the opening. We discovered that three of the "chauffeurs" were women, and when we asked if the women were being abused by being forced to lift the sixty-pound covers the bureau head replied that probably the women's husbands drove the cars although the jobs were listed in the women's names. We discovered that two of the three women were widows, but this did not faze the machine. Actually, the item was a political plum, the jobs going to deserving Democratic precinct captains who were paid $12.50 a day for this service. The cars were used all right, but it was known that at least some precinct captains would hire someone for, say, $5 a day and pocket the remainder. And a Democratic majority in the City Council, accustomed to having its own way, not only beat down our amendment but proceeded to raise the pay of the chauffeurs to $15 per day just to show us who was boss (as if we needed to know)!

On February 8, 1952, several months after this first budget fight, something happened which finally and firmly shaped the course of events. A minor Republican politician and ward committeeman named Gross was shot down in gangland fashion on the city streets, presumably killed by Chicago's mob for reasons unknown. He had operated a handbook (horse betting) for a number of years, and seemed to be moving in the twilight zone of crime and politics. The newspapers discovered that Gross had borrowed money from his Democratic opposite number, and had worked on the staff of the alderman's City Council committee. Our economy bloc, supported by an indignant press and public, forced an ordinance through the City Council establishing a committee to investigate the alliance between organized crime and politics in the city. And because of the civic uproar we won strong representation on this investigating committee. We were able to select a competent counsel and the most stormy investigation in Chicago's history was launched despite an undercurrent of strong opposition from a majority of the City Council (some of whom were mentioned during the course of the investigation), the mayor (who felt that this was a reflection on his administration, although it was never suggested that he or his police commissioner was involved), and later the Democratic state's attorney.

A by-product of the Gross murder was the formation of a

new citizens' group, called the Citizens of Greater Chicago. This group decided to fight for a program of civic reform, emphasizing organizational or structural changes in the city's government and shying away from any direct political action except for a get-out-the-vote campaign prior to each election. The program of the Citizens of Greater Chicago included the reduction in size of the City Council and the transfer to the mayor of some of the administrative powers the Council exercised; the revision of the judicial system in the state and county; the strengthening of civil service, and so forth. Many of the local Democratic leaders resisted these proposals and they were successful in defeating all attempts to get legislative authorization for a referendum on the portion which required voter sanction.

All this, coupled with Democratic opposition to the mayor's civil service commissioner and his program, attempts on the part of Democratic machine aldermen to sabotage the purchasing act of the city by overruling the purchasing agent and giving contracts to favored bidders, were convincing evidence that no change of heart had taken place in Democratic party leaders, despite their election-time support of Mayor Kennelly. It was apparent to me that the machine had been in power too long and had grown fat and indolent. Some of the machine aldermen were arrogant in their power and seemed to delight in flouting public opinion. They derided citizen action, harassed groups appearing before the City Council, and generally acted in a manner designed to discourage effective citizen interest in government (including refusal to allow broadcasting or televising of City Council meetings).

A DECISION IS NEEDED

Compressing eight years in the bawdy setting of Chicago politics into a few pages does injustice to a fascinating story. For three years the crime committee quarreled, investigated, and was frustrated. I became chairman of the committee in

1954 when it was reconstituted following an Illinois Supreme Court decision upholding its legality.

As far back as 1953, some responsible independent citizens of Chicago had talked with me about running for mayor. I was not coy enough to be uninterested, but I was politically educated enough to know the obstacles to such a candidacy. Nevertheless I told this group that I would consider the possibility if serious interest was shown by the citizens of the city. During 1954 an informal group, which called itself Citizens For A Better Chicago (ABC), was organized, raised limited funds, and began the task of building an independent citizens movement.

This *ad hoc* group spent nearly $20,000 in the preliminary period to reprint various speeches of mine and distribute them, to hire a staff of three persons who became field organizers, and to establish an office. This was risk money of the highest order, because there was neither a candidate nor a party—just an idea. A handful of dedicated citizens quietly did this job singlehanded, usually by saying quite honestly to a small group of carefully selected persons: "Do you have some money you would like to throw away on the outside chance that a fellow like Merriam could be elected mayor of Chicago?" Despite many obstacles and the forming lines of a congressional and state campaign (1954), this feat was achieved without fanfare or publicity.

During this same period some of my Republican aldermanic colleagues and some of their party friends, with my knowledge but without my agreement to run, began sounding out Republican party leaders to see if they would support an independent for mayor. The governor and other elected Republican officials were approached, but there was at first almost universal resistance to the idea of backing a candidate who had once been a registered Democrat. However, in the election of November 2, 1954, the Republican ticket in Cook County was swamped, despite the fact that the suburban and rural parts of the county usually vote heavily Republican. In Chicago the Democratic ticket won by approximately 400,000 votes. Not only was the Republican defeat a crushing one but the loss of county offices meant the loss of many jobs which had been filled with the party faithful who had served as the bulwark of the Republican precinct organizations. The recriminations among the Republicans were great, and demoralization was complete.

Such were the circumstances on November 3, 1954, the day after election. Blessed with a friendly press and widespread support from many citizens throughout the city who wanted a clean sweep and who had become organized through the Citizens For A Better Chicago; endowed with a keen interest in the tremendous problems of the liveliest city in the country; trained to be a public administrator; and with broad interests as well as varied ambitions—I was faced with a dilemma. I had at first hand seen my city government wallow in indecision, graft, inefficiency, and tangled governments in its attempts to cope with almost unbelievable problems. And I was attracted by the opportunity to tackle some of those problems with the know-how of modern public administration. Yet political realism, derived from a family history of eight previous political campaigns, taught me caution.

Determined not to move ahead simply "by guess and by golly," my supporters had already contracted for a scientific study to aid in making the decision. In October of 1954 a sampling had been taken in fifty-four neighborhoods of people's views concerning the problems of Chicago, acquaintance with various names being considered as candidates for mayor, and "winter sweepstakes" preferences. This survey was a major factor in my eventual decision to run for office. It showed that next to Kennelly, Merriam was the best known of all persons being considered as candidates in either party. It indicated that I had about as many friends as Kennelly but fewer enemies (natural for one who has not been in the office under question). It also indicated that my strength was being drawn from all three major sources of votes—Republicans, Democrats, and those who classified themselves as independents. The danger signal was the fact that over twice as many Chicagoans classified themselves as Democrats as called themselves Republicans.

The days following the November 1954 election were busy and confused. One of our independent citizens' groups had a well-attended rally at which they urged me to be a candidate for mayor and resolved to form a Citizens-for-Merriam organization throughout the city. Three other wards held similar meetings, and a citywide group was formed. The newspaper editors were seen one by one. The friendliest said that under no circumstances would he support an independent or third-party candidate for mayor. Another urged me to support Kennelly. One was friendly but noncommittal. A fourth was aloof. Meetings were held with a combined group of Citizens For A Better Chicago and Republican aldermen and several ward committeemen. Finally it was agreed that if six Republican ward committeemen could be committed in advance, the combined group would enter me as a candidate in the Republican primary, with or without the support of the Republican organization in Chicago. The candidacy was to be a fusion effort within the Republican primary, with important appeals to independent and Democratic voters as well.

On November 20, 1954, I announced that I would run in the Republican primary as an independent candidate with no commitments other than in the local election.

THE PRIMARY—WE STRESS
ORGANIZATION AND STRATEGY

In one sense the decision of November 20 gave me a feeling of relief. The decision was made; I knew what I was going to do and looked forward to the opportunity of presenting a constructive program for the city's betterment. We had the nucleus of a good independent citizens' organization in a number of wards in the city, some strong and loyal Republican supporters with the possibility of the Republican organization backing, and the possibility of support from the Independent Voters of Illinois, the largest and most effective independent citizens' organization in the city. These three diverse components eventually became the basic units of our campaign force.

A number of things had to be done at once. We had to get an office and a campaign manager. We had to find a finance chairman and get some money. We had to find volunteer workers, give them something to do, and organize them into cohesive ward units. We had to plan an advertising, publicity, and television campaign. We had to get organized political support. And we had to plan strategy. One of my staunchest supporters, Paul Berger, who helped organize our field forces, once said that we had three campaigns at once: the headquarters campaign, the field organization, and the television campaign.

Headquarters Campaign

The headquarters campaign started the day after my announcement. We located some large downtown office space, installed a switchboard and several people, and then waited. We had allowed plenty of room for expansion, and there were times in those early days when the few people there rattled around. But gradually a team shaped up. A loyal friend with some free time on his hands took over management of the office as well as the hundred and one details involved in organizing and setting up a large headquarters. We found the men we wanted for publicity. We asked our friends in television to begin thinking about the campaign. And, vitally important, after some delay we found the man we wanted for campaign manager. Bill Fetridge was a successful businessman, civic leader, and a prominent Republican with a knack for getting along with all kinds of people—a much needed ingredient in this fusion campaign. We found a finance chairman, George McKibben, a former Republican mayoralty candidate. We developed a citizens' committee, basic literature, campaign posters and billboards, and various letterheads, and were then stocked with some of the basic ingredients of a headquarters campaign. The next thing we had to do was to get support to supplement the few ward organizations of ABC; the enlarged group became the Citizens-for-Merriam.

In November of 1954 there was a vacuum in the Republican ranks because of the severe beating the Republicans had taken in the November election. The decision to announce my candidacy on November 20 had been taken in order to enter the void before anyone else could come forward or other forces coalesce. But then came the difficult job of meeting with and getting support from Republican committeemen in the various wards. I called on most of the committeemen personally (with exceptions to be noted later) and solicited their support. Governor Stratton was approached; he indicated that he would not object to my candidacy and, in fact, would encourage action by the Republican Central Committee in support of it.

The Republican city chairman, Ed Moore, who went to Florida to recuperate from the November beating and to escape the early cross-currents in the mayoralty jockeying, finally returned and had a long conference with the governor. Moore, a veteran of political wars, decided to appoint a slate-making committee of ward committeemen and to invite all potential candidates and their friends to appear before the committee. His philosophy was to encourage the candidacy of any regular Republican; but he did not believe that anyone else could indicate any sign of strength. Various combinations of forces were at work to block my endorsement by the Republican organization, but none could coalesce. Lengthy hearings of the Republican slatemaking committee were held, and finally, during Christmas week, I received the endorsement of the Republican Party of Chicago.

There were some difficult matters to consider during this period—the two most thorny being the question of political patronage and its handling if I were elected, and the question of what I would do politically after election (particularly as far as the 1956 election was concerned). The patronage question involved the old problem of how a political party recruits needed workers. The traditional method for many years was through the spoils system, the name derived from the famous comment of the Andrew Jackson era: "To the victors belong the spoils." Chicago is one of the last large cities where spoils politics still continues to play a preeminent role. And both parties have played the patronage game. Aside from my basic belief in the merit system of employee selection, I was also faced with a practical problem: Democrats who were for me were not anxious to have me win and then turn the non-civil service jobs over to the Republican organization to strengthen them in future national elections. And Republican ward committeemen were reluctant to support a candidate who would not help them build up their organizations.

I decided early that I was going to meet this difficult question head on. I told the Republican committeemen that I was making no promises to anyone on the subject of patronage but that obviously I was going to see that such temporary (non-civil service) jobs as there were did not go to those who had opposed me. I also pointed out that effective enforcement of the civil service laws, to which I was unalterably dedicated, would mean that many Democratic precinct captains then doing political work in violation of the spirit, if not the letter, of the law would be held accountable for their political activities.

Field Organization

While this maneuvering was going on, the volunteer

citizens' movement was being welded together. There were continuous problems, particularly in developing cooperation between the amateurs and the "pros." The professionals are traditionally suspicious of the amateurs, and afraid of future competition for control of party machinery. They look with disfavor on any organized group but their own. On the other hand, the amateurs are often suspicious of the professionals, afraid of double-dealing or "trading with the enemy," doubtful because of the professionals' cynicism, and impatient with their lack of zeal. To balance these two points of view most effectively, the zeal of the volunteer should be used to augment the know-how of the professional. The best precinct work is done by someone who knows the people on whom he is calling. A good professional politician makes it his business to know his people, and he calls on them between elections as well as during them. This is the real secret of a successful machine—its men are always available and helpful to their people. Good professionals combined with energetic amateurs provide a strong striking force. However, it became clear early in this campaign that the volunteers and the professionals would have to operate separately. We set up liaison between the two as best we could, and I informed all the Republican ward committeemen that I was asking the volunteer groups to check in with the professionals at periodic intervals.

The job of the twelve full-time paid field workers in the Citizens-for-Merriam organization was to ferret out potential leaders in the volunteer movement, train them, and encourage them to find volunteer precinct workers. Then the task was to keep everyone working, give them literature, keep them up to date on the issues, and generally direct their activities. When one realizes that there are over four thousand precincts in Chicago, the size of this task becomes apparent. Citizens-for-Merriam estimated that over two thousand of these precincts were actually canvassed by working volunteers by the end of the campaign. In all, probably something over three thousand volunteers were working in these precincts and in the various offices.

Any such huge volunteer activity is a major undertaking; this one was especially formidable since most of the people had never even pushed a political doorbell before. The first step had to be an educational program to acquaint them with the political facts of life. A manual for precinct workers was developed, and films demonstrating how to work a precinct were shown to many groups. The volunteers were taught how to register a voter, how to watch the polls on election day, and how to ring a doorbell. The more bashful were encouraged to work in pairs until they had overcome their shyness. "Coffee sips" throughout the city were a fertile recruiting ground for workers, as were numerous independent citizens' ward rallies and personal contacts by the volunteer ward leaders. The most difficult job, we discovered, was to find competent persons to assume leadership in recruiting volunteer workers.

Television Campaign

A major part of the campaign effort was allocated to television programs. We devoted a great deal of energy and money to this television effort. Here was the largest single medium for reaching the voters directly with personal appeals for support. I was known to television viewers, as the result of a series of programs which WGN-TV had sponsored in 1954 called "Spotlight on Chicago." It was this series that had helped to bring about a special grand jury inquiry into organized crime. The same devoted people who had helped put together "Spotlight on Chicago" were utilized to develop our television campaign. The main ingredient was a thirteen-week series of Sunday-night programs. Each of these programs was devoted to a specific topic: housing and neighborhood conservation, traffic, organized crime, fusion, and so forth. They were dramatic presentations rather than speeches, and their effectiveness was best demonstrated by the fact that most of the other candidates in the primaries began to follow our format (until one week we shifted gears and televised an old-fashioned political rally, which nobody else had dared try). The audience rating on this series indicated that at least 200,000 sets a week tuned in on the program.

In addition to the thirteen-week series, we had a one-hour election-eve roundup; a ten-minute question-and-answer program for me every weekday and evening for three weeks; a five-minute noontime show with Mrs. Merriam which was carried three times a week for three weeks (she invited me as her guest on one show); and 125 spot announcements.

Our television campaign was geared to compete with other shows to capture the viewer's interest. We tried to make an impact without being "smooth," but we were always conscious of the fact that a dull speech would quickly lose an audience. Judging by the number of comments we received, television was an effective weapon.

Hazards of fusion

Our broad strategy in the primary was fairly simple. First, we had to convince large numbers of Chicagoans that this was, in fact, a local election, that national issues were not involved, and that it should be decided on the basis of the candidates and the local issues. We were fighting a big and deeply entrenched machine, which had all the money it wanted, probably ten thousand patronage jobs, and control of the police, election machinery, and law enforcement officers. We were also faced with the obvious fact, convincingly demonstrated in the previous election, that the majority of Chicagoans, all other things being equal, were Democrats.

Even in its early stages, the Committee For A Better Chicago had grappled with this problem. The members of this committee determined in 1954 that they were interested in a good candidate for mayor regardless of political affiliation. Its leaders were for Merriam whatever route he took. At one time consideration was given to the relative merit of running in the party primaries as contrasted to running as an independent candidate in the election, thus skipping the primaries. Serious study was given to the La Guardia movement in New York. However, an immediate obstacle was found in the election laws of Illinois, which precluded the New York pattern where one person's name could appear under several column headings. For example, La Guardia was the candidate of both the Republican and Fusion parties and his name appeared on the ballot in two places. Practically, this meant that those Democrats or Independents who wanted to vote for La Guardia but did not want to vote Republican even in a local election had some place to make their X. But in Illinois a candidate could file on only one ticket. This practical obstacle proved one of the most difficult in the campaign.

Once the decision was made to run in the Republican primary, we turned to item number one in our strategy: to try to educate people to an understanding of the local character of this campaign. This was no easy task, and quite obviously the strategy of the opposition was to say the opposite and to try to hold the allegiance of all people who ordinarily voted Democratic in Chicago. This problem was further complicated by the necessity of getting the traditional Republican voters to support this novel idea and vote for me. The opposition exploited our dilemma at every turn.

Continually throughout the campaign we placed our emphasis on fusion. In March, after the primary, support of me by the Independent Voters of Illinois (an independent group which had usually supported Democratic candidates) added weight to this argument, as did the support of Frank Keenan, Democratic ward committeeman and the elected county assessor, who had supported Mayor Kennelly in the primary. A Democrats-for-Merriam committee was established to further emphasize the bipartisan nature of the campaign. And

most of our field staff were Democrats in their personal leanings.

But in order to solidify the Republican supporters (de-
moralized and unhappy as a result of the November election),
a decision was made which a few political analysts think had
widespread repercussions. Some of my advisers felt that it
would be better if the Republican organization did not
endorse me at all in the primary and fought me with either
token or real opposition. Another group of consultants believed
that it would be better to have no primary opposition so that
I would have time to solidify my Republican support, become
acquainted with the membership of the many ward organizations, and be better prepared for the main bout following the
primary. This latter school of thought prevailed, and thus
there was no substantial primary opposition. Some analysts
contended that this was a mistake—that it made me appear
to be the Republican organization candidate.

Another aspect of our campaign to stress fusion was my
statement to both the Republican and Democratic supporters
that I would not use the office of mayor for national partisan
purposes. This attitude seemed to be necessary for bipartisan
support in a key state the year before an important presidential election, particularly since many of my friends were
ardent Stevenson boosters. My contention was that the office
of mayor of the City of Chicago was a full-time job and that I
would not use the prestige of the mayor's position for either
side in the national election. Although there had been prece-
dent for this in other cities, and even in the actions of
Mayor Kennelly (who always remained more or less aloof
from national politics), still it was difficult for Republicans to
accept this from someone running on their ticket, and it was
hard for some Democrats to believe that I would stick by my
agreement (although I was determined to do so). The Democratic machine hit hard at this point, their contention being

that my position was a subterfuge to clothe a traditional Republican candidate in sheep's clothing.

Another major item of strategy revolved around the position which I should take concerning the Democratic primary fight. The Democratic primary had three major candidates: the incumbent Mayor Kennelly; Richard Daley, county clerk, ward committeeman, and chairman of the Democratic Party of Chicago and Cook County; and Benjamin Adamowski, a prominent Polish-American leader, formerly Mayor Kennelly's corporation counsel, and for some years previously a member of the state legislature.

Mayor Kennelly had gained the enmity of many politicians because of his aloof stand on matters of party concern: in particular by his actions in strengthening city civil service so that the number of temporary jobs available to the Democratic organization had been cut from eighteen thousand to three thousand; by his refusal to accept certain recommendations of Negro Democratic leaders; and by his failure to reappoint a CIO official to the Board of Education. Sensing an opportunity to capitalize on the good achievements of the Kennelly administration and at the same time restore direct control of the party organization over city hall, the Democratic city central committee determined that they would drop Kennelly and slate a new candidate. It was their hope that Mayor Kennelly would not contest this action and that he would retire gracefully. As a part of this process, a slatemaking committee of the Democratic ward committeemen was selected to interview potential candidates. The mayor appeared before the committee and spoke for less than three minutes on the achievements of his administration in asking the Democratic slatemakers' endorsement. No questions were asked and the mayor was told that the interview was ended. Mayor Kennelly decided to fight, and announced his candidacy in the Democratic primary even before the slatemaking committee had acted. The slatemakers subsequently picked the man who had picked them (Daley, county chairman and reelected as county clerk one month previous) as the organization's candidate for mayor.

All four Chicago papers hopped into the primary fray on Kennelly's side and, although they had all at one time or another been critical of his inaction in some fields, they began an intensive campaign of support for him. Only two of the fifty Democratic committeemen supported the mayor, but he initiated a vigorous campaign, denouncing the "boys in the Morrison" (the hotel which housed the headquarters of the Democratic forces). Daley's strategy was to remain quiet and try to avoid controversy as much as possible.

This was the problem with which my advisers and I wrestled at great length. Should I ignore the Democratic primary and just talk about issues? Should I attack all the Democratic candidates? Should I concentrate all my fire at this time on Mr. Daley, the organization candidate? The press urged me to attack Daley and the machine. But this might nominate Kennelly, who most people believed would be a harder candidate to beat. And it must be remembered that while I had supported Mayor Kennelly on many issues, I had also criticized his lack of action in other respects, particularly where finances and police-crime tieups were involved.

I decided to concentrate on a positive program of presenting issues, particularly on our television programs. But this received little attention in the press because they were absorbed in the Kennelly-Daley fight. I implicitly criticized the mayor by pointing out how powerful the office of mayor could be. This was necessitated by the widespread belief, stemming from Kennelly's own actions and an impression spread by some well-meaning citizens wanting a new city charter, that the mayor had little power to solve Chicago's many problems. I pointed out that not only did the mayor have a veto power, which Kennelly had never used, but on the budget he had an item veto which was a greater power than the President of the United States could exercise. I also attacked the machine and the Chicago system of government by favoritism and worse, and said that whoever the Democratic candidate would be, it made no difference to the welfare of Chicago so long as the system was in effect. And I ridiculed the "draft" of Daley by himself.

Would it have made any difference if I had launched into an all-out attack on Daley and the Democratic organization in the primary and, in effect, joined up with Kennelly in an attack from several directions? Could I have gone to Kennelly and offered this kind of help if Kennelly had agreed to support me if he lost the primary? As events turned out, Kennelly, who on primary night almost declared his support of me, finally decided to sit out the election. And despite a personal conference between us, he did not support me.

The primary ended with a Daley victory of about 100,000 plurality over Kennelly. I received just over 100,000 votes in an extremely light Republican primary vote. The main bout was on and my immediate problem was to gain the initiative, keep the opposition off guard, and exploit its weaknesses.

FORTY-TWO DAYS IN THE LIFE OF A CANDIDATE

As I quietly sit and write of the final lap of the campaign— those forty-two days from primary to election—events form and fade as in a kaleidoscope. There were touching moments: The many friends who gave of their time, energy, and money because they believed in me; the enthusiasm of young people getting interested in politics for the first time; the thousands of people one met—of every race, color, and creed—at a Polish dance, a Czech patriotic rally, a St. Patrick's Day luncheon, at Sunday service in a Negro Baptist church, at a healing session interrupted for my political talk (the most difficult moment of the campaign). Then, too, there are memories of the grueling days.

A *Candidate in Motion*

The demands upon a candidate almost defy description. A reliable speedometer on a station-wagon-turned-house (complete with electric razor and almost all the comforts of home) clocked six thousand miles (all within the city) in forty-two days. The nerve-wracking dash from place to place would have shaken the equanimity of most human beings. The difficulties in scheduling meetings in a city of 211 square miles sometimes seemed insurmountable. We were convinced, my driver and I, that some diabolical force was making up our schedule, placing each successive meeting at the furthermost point from the previous one. But we prided ourselves on missing only two meetings, and those on a snowy, slick night.

Each morning the office handed us our orders for the day. The schedule included meetings with delegations (of all sorts and varieties), coffee sips, lunch with advisers or representatives of other groups that had to be seen, a press conference, shaking hands at a plant gate or in the neighborhoods, the daily ten-minute question-and-answer television program, rallies for the party faithful or citizen groups in the evening, joint appearances with my opponent before nonpartisan audiences (until he started sending substitutes), and sometimes midnight strategy conferences on subjects of importance. At midnight or later I dragged my feet up the steps of our house and spent a few tired moments with my wife and youngest child, who had to be awakened to get a late bottle (often this was the only time I saw the baby).

Photographers and reporters followed me constantly. Pictures were taken of father feeding the baby at 6:00 A.M. (taken at 8:30 A.M.), mother feeding the baby at 6:00 P.M., the entire family (whenever it could be gathered), mother putting the baby to bed, father and mother doing the dishes, the children helping around the house. And even on election night, after defeat, the photographers awaited my departure from campaign headquarters to catch a picture of me putting the key in the door. The next morning they were there once more to get a family shot of how the defeated candidate gets re-acquainted with his family. (Or perhaps they wanted to see if the candidate was still alive: On election night I went to bed about 1:30 A.M., dead to the world—figuratively at least. Nearly an hour later the doorbell rang vigorously until my wife was finally awakened to find five squads of police and a supervisor's car in front of the house—they had received a phone call that there had been a shooting at our address. Was it wishful thinking?)

The woman's page reporters descended on my wife, wanting to know the intimate details of our family life, favorite recipes, my little-known habits, and the like. The candidate's wife was expected to put in appearances as a guest on television programs, at banquets and teas, and other such affairs. And despite the fact that we had a small baby, my wife finally felt impelled to pitch in and make citywide appearances at the Citizens-for-Merriam coffee sips.

There are other not so pleasant aspects in the life of a candidate's family. There were days when I did not see my oldest daughter at all. Our son's grades in school began to slip. Both of the school-age children wondered if they were making friends because of the campaign and their father, or because of themselves. When we went into the race, I sat down with my entire family and told them what to expect in a political campaign. I told them that there would undoubtedly be momentary hurts, and that they should expect to hear lots of things about their father (and perhaps themselves) during the course of the campaign. Because of our talk they were at least partially prepared for what followed.

The attempts to defame came in various ways. The state's attorney diligently worked on a false lead from an ex-convict implying that I had taken money from a gambler in return for a promise of protection. Later he incorrectly contended that I had tried to have the mayor indicted. He also claimed that nothing of importance in the way of crime-politics tieups had been presented to the grand jury. He ignored the fact that the grand jury in a rare action had extended its term an extra month to weigh the information which was presented to it.

On another occasion I ended up seemingly as the accused in the trial of a city building inspector who had been arrested as the result of information given by me to the state's attorney. A lady building owner in my ward had come to see me one day charging that she had been approached by an inspector who told her that for a sum of money he would ignore her building violations. (As chairman of the housing committee of the City Council I had been instrumental in adding personnel to the department to cope with the many violations and illegal conversions of buildings in my ward and elsewhere, and this inspector was one of those added as a result of these efforts.) We were uncertain about her story, and decided to see if evidence could for once be obtained against an inspector suspected of corruption. (The building commissioner said he could never get *facts*.) We stationed my assistant, Robert Stierer, with a wire recorder and a cameraman from *Life* Magazine (they had been assigned that week to do a picture story of my TV series) in the basement of the lady's apartment. The inspector arrived, and a recording and pictures were made as he offered his proposition. The lady asked him to come back the next day, and we called the state's attorney to tell him of the attempt. The next day the state's attorney's men were present when the inspector returned; they arrested him while he was in her apartment, but the case was delayed for months, until the mayoralty campaign was on. Then the defense agreed to go to trial. I was put on the stand and grilled by the defense attorney who contended that the whole episode was a publicity stunt on my part. The inspector was acquitted of the bribery charge but later convicted of carrying a concealed weapon (he was armed when arrested).

The opposition claimed that this episode proved I was only a publicity seeker, and further said that it showed I would turn on anyone to gain an advantage. (The inspector, it turned out, was a Democratic precinct captain whom I had known from my own ward.) Such was the result of one attempt to uncover fraud in a vital city service.

Two actions should have left their perpetrators deeply ashamed. During World War II my college romance and early marriage became a wartime casualty. Although there were no children of this marriage and nothing unpleasant to report except that apparently I was gone too long during the war, the opposition tried to arouse prejudiced people against me, particularly on religious grounds. While the idea of divorce is repugnant to me, it is not forbidden by my religion and I did not attempt to stand in my wife's way when she asked to be free. Despite these facts, letters were sent out saying no one knew how many wives I had or how many children I was failing to support. Photostatic copies of the divorce papers were circulated, particularly in some convents. And some enterprising person, presumably an opposition supporter, conceived the notion of stealing the divorce papers from the county courthouse in western Illinois where my wife had lived. This evoked a story on the wire services, the implication being that I had had the papers removed to prevent some scandal from coming out. The week following election the county clerk announced that the papers had been returned in a blank envelope. "At least they should have thanked me for them," he told the local newspaper.

The second action was what the trade calls a "roarback." It was used with some success, I believe, in the last few days of the campaign. It was a letter written on the purported letterhead of the American Negro Civic Association, a fictitious organization, urging all recipients of the letter to vote for Merriam because he would see that Negroes could move to all parts of the city and would find sites on which they could build housing. This letter was sent to the white areas of the city, where no Negroes were living, in a blatant effort to arouse racial prejudices.

Another phony letter by a fictitious Eisenhower-Taft League called on all Republicans to reject Merriam because of alleged previous association with left-wingers. Still another was put on every car in one ward, purportedly signed by an aldermanic candidate friendly to me, saying, "I agree with Robert E. Merriam in stopping overnite street parking." This was a particularly touchy issue in some neighborhoods and incidentally an issue on which I had not taken a stand. The friendly candidate sent out a crew the same night the cards were distributed and dumped over five thousand of them on my desk, having picked them up before they were seen by the car owners.

The Communist Party of Chicago, indicating that it still had not lost its technique (or influence), not only got out a pamphlet of its own denouncing Merriam as an enemy of the people but apparently duped other groups into issuing almost identical pamphlets containing the same charges. And one Republican ward committeeman, whose support I had rejected, issued a fancy pamphlet in support of Daley that was full of misrepresentations.

Dozens of people were willing to give me the one idea which could win the election. Most of them just *had* to talk to me personally. One never knows when a good idea may come along, but the time factor was such that I told each one that if he did not think his idea could survive being passed through someone else's hands to reach me, it could not be good enough. Who knows? I may have thrown away the idea of the century in rejecting the approaches of those who would speak only to me. One friend, however, did get my ear with his plan (and the idea had been used successfully, I believe, in the past). He told me that he was prepared to arrange either a time bomb in my car motor or a shotgun-spraying of the car while I was riding in it! When I looked at him in some alarm, he assured me that it could be so timed that I would not be harmed. I think he is still disappointed that I was not willing to go through with this, and he still believes it could have won the election.

These are a few memories of forty-two hectic days. I cannot begin to count the number of speeches I made. I would not hazard a guess as to how many hands I shook (although my elbow still aches reminiscently). And I could not possibly recreate the alternating exhilaration and depression of a candidate at work. But I would not have missed the experience for anything.

A Working Organization Is Formed

The personal campaign is a small but important part of any election; more vital was the development of our working organization. First of all, with the lines clearly drawn we could step up our recruiting of volunteer personnel. We tried to pick up as much of the Kennelly support as possible (with considerable success). More groups were formed—Veterans for Merriam, Japanese-Americans for Merriam, Kennelly Democrats for Merriam, Churchmen for Merriam, Women for Merriam, Youth for Merriam, and so forth.

We intensified our volunteer precinct activities, and drew in many recruits. We had all kinds of help. School children, sometimes led by my own, came down to help address letters, stamp envelopes, or fold literature, and so forth. At all hours of the day, and most of the night, volunteers were at work at headquarters. Dozens of volunteers in the last weeks of the campaign engaged in a massive telephone campaign in which over 200,000 people were called. Sound trucks roamed the streets. Some friends with trucks put big signs on them. Several torchlight parades were held (my daughter ended up in a neighbor's backyard on a horse the Saturday before

election). The volunteer offices had rallies, passed out literature, recruited workers.

And always there was the backbone of any campaign—the
workers in the precincts, the Republican precinct captains
supplemented wherever possible by our volunteer precinct
workers and those of the Independent Voters of Illinois.

The coffee sips in many parts of the city proved to be a
highly effective campaign technique. They brought into the
Citizens-for-Merriam organization dozens of women who had
never been active before. I had always felt that women were
the key to an effective citizens political action movement.
They can find more time (although many of them, including
my wife, reminded me that they were quite busy with family
and home throughout the day); they are good organizers
when once started; they are vitally affected by many local
problems and municipal actions; and they are not as cynical as
their business or working husbands who see corruption or
influence-peddling at work too often in their daily activities.
In those areas where a good job was done the role of the
women in getting out the vote was noticeable.

The pattern of questions at coffee sips and other such
gatherings was almost always the same: Could anything really
be done about Chicago? How could I as an individual fight
city hall? Or, weren't they all crooks? (Mysteriously, I used
to become somewhat indignant at this one.) My stock answer
was to remind the women that since the suffrage amendment
had been enacted the percentage of people participating in
elections had steadily declined (except for 1952 when the
women elected Eisenhower), and that the women were the
ones most neglectful of their right to vote. "Of course, I don't
mean to imply you shouldn't have the right to vote," I said,
"only that you should *use* the right you fought so hard to
obtain." And a stock conclusion was, "Never underestimate the
power of a woman—if she gets mad. But what does it take to
get the women stirred up?"

In some wards of the city, particularly outlying residential wards, they did get stirred up. In one ward the incumbent alderman (a Republican) squeezed through by several hundred votes, while I won by fifteen thousand. The difference represented a variety of factors, but the women, with their coffee sips, doorbell ringing, talking, and mailing of literature, were an important part.

But articulate, energetic help such as we obtained comes generally from the more prosperous areas where patterns of activity, interest, and understanding have been established through education and training (even if the habits have fallen into disuse in far too many cases). What does one do in the depressed areas of the city where people are preoccupied with just existing, where there are few, if any, community organizations? Here the problem of reaching the potential voter and worker is a difficult one. Coffee sips were held in the Negro areas of the city, and one lady did a yeoman's job in trying to stir up extensive interest. But it is hard to get people to meetings in such areas; their lives are already crowded and there is no pattern of independent thought or action in politics. For example, when we attempted to hold a meeting in one of the public housing projects, I was told that people were warned by Democratic precinct captains that they would be thrown out of the project if they attended.

With what I thought was an important message—a vigorous record of fighting against discrimination and for better housing, as opposed to my opponent who, many thought, had been less than forthright on these issues—I was confronted with a lack of communication means. The Republican organization in some of the inner wards of the city was openly hostile, in others, weak. Television, radio, and the newspapers did not have the impact they had in outlying residential wards. Without independent citizen activities, which never took root on a large scale in these wards, how did one tell his story? We pondered this at various strategy meetings.

One answer, but it could only be an incomplete one in a city the size of Chicago, was personal contact. Sometimes I got out of the station wagon and started walking down a street in the heart of the Negro area, just introducing myself and shaking hands with everyone I could. At plant gates I shook hundreds and hundreds of hands of the men coming on and off the shifts until a callus grew on my right little finger and bursitis (which months later was still with me) afflicted my elbow. From then on each handshake was painful.

Money problems

One aspect of political campaigns that nobody likes to think about is the vexsome problem of financing. When I was first asked to consider being a candidate for mayor this was one of the questions to which I gave early serious consideration. Those in the know said that it would cost $500,000 to wage a good campaign in the city of Chicago. Where was such a sum to come from?

Some $20,000 had been raised in the uncertain period before I was a candidate, but financing the main effort was another matter. Overhead was high because it was necessary to have a staff of organizers mobilizing and directing the large group of volunteer precinct and citizen workers. At its peak this entailed the work of twelve full-time field workers, sixteen offices and their staffs in various parts of the city, and, in addition, the central office and its staff. The 200,000 telephone calls by 300 volunteers and other expenses brought the total telephone bill to $23,000. Printing costs were $65,000, and advertising expenses were $95,000. This included $35,000 for television, $16,000 for radio (28 five-minute and 690 one-minute spot announcements), $22,000 for billboard space in 320 locations, and newspaper advertising totaling $4,000, to mention the major items. The largest single item of expenditure was $116,930 given to the Republican city central committee for financing precinct activities on primary and election days (at the rate of $5 per precinct captain on primary day and $25 per precinct captain on election day).

The total of actual cash expenditures in the campaign, primary and election, including the small amount of risk money in precampaign days, was $409,710.32, coming all too close to the original estimate of $500,000. When donated services were added to the cash outlay, the figure was even closer to that mark. The best available estimate is that the winning Democrats spent well over $1 million.

How is such a sum of money raised, and what do the contributors expect from their investment? Actually, in this campaign over three thousand individual contributors participated, from a low of ten cents provided by an elementary school girl to a contribution of well in excess of $10,000. All the traditional means of raising money were employed: direct mail solicitation, personal calls, and a fundraising dinner which netted over $80,000. However, the one part of fundraising which was neglected was a large-scale campaign for small contributions, which I wanted to try but which never got off the ground except in our volunteer citizen ward groups when the hat was passed.

Some contributors of substantial sums obviously gave to both candidates to insure, so they hoped, fair treatment of their interests no matter who was elected. Generally these were interests having, at some point, direct contact with the city. Some contributors hoped to have a friend in court in time of need, and my position was always that "if you have legitimate business with the city, I'll never penalize you for having helped me; but don't count on any special assistance." Because of my fight on organized crime, no direct approaches were made by the syndicate (which has been a potent influence in the Chicago area). But one man representing himself as part of a racket which was being invaded by the syndicate let it be known through an intermediary that he was willing to raise $50,000 from his associates, not on the guarantee of protection from the law, but on the understanding that the syndicate would be "taken off their back." This sum was not accepted.

Despite the most rigid of economy steps, which prevented our doing many things we had hoped to do, and despite the multifold fundraising activities, the week before election found us with no money for election-day purposes. My campaign manager, the Republican county chairman, and I met in serious conference to determine how to find the money to finish the campaign. At the eleventh hour a great citizen offered to borrow, on his signature, $67,000 with which to meet these needs. Not many people are willing, unselfishly, wanting nothing whatever for themselves, to take that kind of risk! This loan and $33,000 of unpaid bills were a legacy from the campaign. A postelection banquet (eight hundred people at $50 per plate feted the defeated candidate) helped to defray part of that cost. I was overwhelmed by the turnout. As the governor himself said at the banquet, "There are times when I haven't been able to get anyone to buy me a hamburger when I lost."

Key strategy

During all this time our strategy program continued to evolve. Here are some of the major issues we developed.

1. *Vote frauds* unfortunately have been a perennial problem in Chicago. Although they are much talked about, little in the way of remedial action seemed to have been taken. And the election machinery was in the hands of the Democratic organization. I determined to see if we could obtain any evidence of actual vote thievery on primary day. We found a man willing to try. This man was disgusted with the Democratic organization and decided to run for alderman against the incumbent. No sooner had he announced his intentions than he was threatened, a gun was pulled on him, and he was told to get out of the race for alderman if he wanted to live.

As he later reported it, he decided he had better get out of the race because he could not get police cooperation. But he came to me with his story and complaint.

This man agreed to go to his usual polling place on primary day, armed with a miniature camera and tape recorder concealed in his coat pocket. There he struck oil. Operating in that precinct on primary day was a gentleman known as "Short-Pencil." (Short-pencilling is the skill of concealing a short pencil in the palm of one's hand, erasing one X and substituting another in the square for an alternate candidate.) My friend took pictures of Short-Pencil at work; he recorded a portion of the conversation during which, he reported, the judge of elections told Short-Pencil to stay away from the ballots; and then, working all night with a lawyer, he drew up a sworn affidavit attesting to all that he had seen. All of this was given to me the morning following the primary and shortly before a City Council meeting which had been called for that day. Here was a real break and evidence of deliberate tampering with the ballots.

I released the story at the City Council meeting, having before then sent copies of the affidavit to the state's attorney and the county judge. The story had enormous impact and was discussed for some days while the Democrats decided what to do with it. The one thing that was not done was to press any action against Short-Pencil. In fact, the complainant was not even called in for some time to tell his version of the story, and in the final analysis the only action taken by the election commissioners was to suspend the members of the election board. We used the incident to illustrate the way in which we believed the machine had maintained itself in power. The issue set the pace for the campaign and gave our forces the offensive, which was never relinquished. (The complainant, incidentally, ended up with a police guard during the campaign, and when it was over he was actually shot at and finally left town for good.)

2. *More fusion?* A second major strategy problem during the election campaign centered around the need for a fusion of forces from all political ranks. Our forces had one entire television program outlining the history of fusion in other cities, explaining and showing how it had worked, and parading a bipartisan group of supporters before the cameras. Mrs. La Guardia was interviewed by me from New York and told her version of the New York fusion effort (which, incidentally, was very similar to the Chicago story and problem). On every public occasion our forces stressed the bipartisan nature of my support. The Daley backers countered with emphasis on party regularity, the importance of the Illinois vote in the 1956 presidential election, the evils of the Republican backers of Merriam, and the importance of a two-party system. "Independent" Daley backers who stressed the need for a Democratic mayor were trotted out.

3. *A gigantic rally?* Another important strategy decision revolved around a morale question. Should our forces have a large rally in the Chicago Stadium (which holds nearly twenty thousand people)? On the positive side I envisaged an all-Chicago rally with emphasis on the constructively heterogeneous nature of Chicago's polyglot population. It was to be a pageant of various nationality-group folk dances and songs. It was an ideal way to encourage participation by these groups which still exist as an important factor in Chicago life.

But what if there was a disappointingly small crowd? The Democrats with all their money, jobs, and power were unwilling to try to fill the stadium in a local campaign. A poor turnout could be a damper on the whole campaign. Bill Fetridge and I finally determined that if we had a small crowd at the stadium we would lose anyway, and that we might as well know about this a week in advance of election day. One newspaper political editor called me to say that I ought to have my head examined if we went through with the stadium meeting. But we decided that this was a risk worth taking.

The cost of the entire rally and publicity was $23,000. A beautiful pageant was arranged, nearly a million tickets were distributed, and an intensive campaign of publicity was launched, particularly on the many foreign-language radio stations and in the foreign-language newspapers. On the night of the rally we went to the stadium with hearts in hand. And as we approached, we noted half-empty parking lots. Nevertheless, inside was a huge crowd, estimated at nearly fifteen thousand persons, comfortably filling most of the stadium. The meeting was a success (except for my speech, I now think—it was given at 10:30 P.M.), and even cynical ward committeemen were enthusiastic at the response. The campaign was given a lift, and we breathed a sigh of relief.

4. *Crime and politics.* Two major issues were held in abeyance for the wind-up of the campaign. The first was the alliance between crime and politics in Chicago. This had been boiling over since the Gross murder. Although the crime committee seemed to have accomplished too little of a tangible nature, more recent activities started under my chairmanship were making progress. But the chief investigator for the committee, dissatisfied with the progress that had been made, had resigned soon after the primaries. Before resigning, however, he had sent a series of memoranda to his superior outlining areas in which public hearings could be held.

One area revolved around a big-shot gambler who had tie-ups with many politicians. It had been discovered during the course of the investigations that this gambler had an ingenious message device—he carried in his pocket a small radio receiver on which he received telephone messages. What the gambler did not know was that FCC regulations require that all such messages be recorded by the agency providing the service. The gambler was operating under an alias and with a call number, so that those calling him *ipso facto* had to know who he was and what he was doing. The committee also knew through other sources what he was doing and where he was conducting his gambling operations. A check of his messages revealed a series of calls from the city hall office of one alderman, from ward headquarters of one Democratic committeeman, from notorious syndicate hoodlums, and so forth. Other unrelated information revealed telephone calls between a prominent politician and Jack Guzik (a syndicate big-shot), tip-offs from police captains to gambling operations which were reported to them by the committee staff, policy operations protected by police, and other tangible signs of crime-police-politics tieups.

How to get the information out in the open? The chief investigator was invited back to Chicago to tell why he had resigned from the committee staff. But the Democratic majority of the crime committee voted that his memoranda should not even be examined by the members of the committee, and his testimony was bottled up in secret session. The state legislature then moved in at our suggestion. In hearings on a bill to give the attorney general the right to take over law enforcement in counties where it had broken down, they quizzed the chief investigator and asked him about his memoranda. A second meeting was held where the memoranda were to be released, but the Democrats on the state senate committee voted to approve the bill (which they had been opposing) to get it out of committee and end the hearings. This unique strategy closed out this avenue for release of the information. Some of the facts were given to the newspapers, and the chief investigator's memoranda were obtained by one paper and published on the Sunday before election, with screaming headlines. And on my final Sunday-night television program I used this information, and personal knowledge of many of these situations, to reveal some of the crime-politics tieups.

One question which all these revelations raised was whether Chicago would become a wide-open town if the Democrats won. By this was meant whether gambling, narcotics, and so forth, would be opened up and allowed to run rampant. There was no doubt that the syndicate and its political henchmen of both parties were not supporting me, and we believed that they were supporting the Democrat, Daley, in both the primary and the election. The gamblers were "rarin' to go," having been harassed in the Kennelly administration. It was reported to us that loudspeaker equipment for horse racing betting handbooks was being readied, and the word in the "profession" was that the town was going to open up. Daley's good personal reputation made this a difficult issue for us to exploit because he had not been personally tied to this element in the Democratic party. But the aims of some of those who engineered the dumping of Kennelly seemed clear, and we exploited this argument. What effect it had on the election is unknown, but many observers agreed that it had a tangible effect.

5. *The "West-Side Bloc."* Another part of strategy development revolved around the so-called "west-side bloc" of wards in Chicago. It was widely believed that in eight wards of the city, there had been a working relationship between elected committeemen of the two parties. The dominant Democrats themselves apparently influenced, and probably named and helped elect, the Republican committeemen. There was strong suspicion in many quarters that a dominant force in these controlled wards was the crime syndicate. The newspapers were particularly critical of the minority (Republican) committeemen and the legislators from these districts in the state legislature, who were dubbed the "west-side bloc" because they stuck together regardless of party affiliation in fighting certain bills designed to strengthen law enforcement procedures in the state and other measures. There was good evidence to support the argument that the Republican committeemen in these wards at general elections would support, or not resist effectively, the Democratic candidates for various offices. And the entire west-side bloc leadership was in public disrepute.

To add to this, as a member and then as chairman of the crime committee I had been unusually vigorous in my opposition to this kind of politics. Yet all but one of the members from these wards voted for my endorsement when my name was submitted to the Republican city central committee for approval.

I determined that we would have a series of luncheon meetings with the various Republican committeemen to pep them up. But I decided that the eight committeemen of the westside bloc would not be invited. Open war was declared and as a result eight wards were left completely uncovered as far as the Republican organization was concerned. The Democrats exploited this by contending that I was anti-Italian, a charge which was pounded home among the thousands of good citizens living in these wards who had no part in the illegal activities. This charge hurt, not only in votes but personally, particularly in view of my own sympathetic interest in all minority groups and my desire to help them create better neighborhoods in which to live.

There were some who said that my rejection of these politicians was a mistake, that I should have accepted support wherever I could find it, or that at least these elected Republican committeemen should not have been openly antagonized. But the election results showed that I lost these eight wards by 100,000 votes, almost the identical margin by which Eisenhower had been beaten in 1952, Senator Dirksen in 1950, and Hoellen (Daley's opponent for county clerk) in 1954, and in none of these elections were the Republican committeemen openly rejected. My calculated risk was that they would be against me no matter what happened, so why have the onus of their tacit support and the probability of their silent opposition.

6. *The "ghosts."* We had had quite a reaction to our revelations of the incident showing vote irregularities. How much more of this could be discovered? It had long been suspected

that many phony registrations were kept on the books, particularly in the west-side wards where there was no effective two-party system. One day I suggested that it might be possible to find out something about the phony registrants if a letter were sent to a sampling of residents of these wards. If Uncle Sam could not find them, we reasoned, it would be logical to presume that they were not there. A mailing of thirty thousand letters was made to registered voters, using a dummy organization name in the corner of the envelope, and enclosing miscellaneous advertising material. Of the thirty thousand letters mailed in a hundred precincts of the city, over three thousand, or about 10 per cent, were returned by the post office as undeliverable. A spot check of these three thousand letters revealed that many of the so-called registrants were from vacant lots, parking lots, some even from the playground of a school, some from a block which was entirely vacant, and so forth. Pictures were taken of some of these locations, and then the entire story given to the newspapers. This sampling was projected to indicate that there might be as many as 100,000 phony names on the registers. The newspapers called these the "ghosts."

This story came out about a week before the election. The answer made by the election commissioners was that most of these names were on the registers because of clerical oversights or because the individuals had recently moved from areas of the city that were being cleared for various public projects (which was the case in some instances, but still did not justify the sloppy bookkeeping).

The battle of the ghosts raged during the entire last week of the campaign. The question, of course, was: "Were the Democratic precinct captains voting any of these ghosts?" Affidavits obtained during the primary indicated that in some instances they were.

One result of all these revelations was that election boards were much more cautious than they otherwise would have been on election day. Tangible evidence of this was the fact that Mr. Daley got twenty thousand less votes in the eight west-side wards on election day in April 1955 than he had only five months before, in November 1954, when an equivalent number of persons had voted. And on election day my campaign manager and I, with two police officers and a lawyer with a huge copy of the statute books under his arm, toured the precincts in the west-side wards to check on election day irregularities.

All this time the strategy of the Democrats was to keep things as quiet as they could, play up the personal record of their candidate, urge people to retain party regularity, and raise doubts in people's minds as to my chances. One particularly inventive propaganda line was quite successful in many areas. Some Democratic precinct captains told their voters that if they had voted in the Democratic primary they could not vote for me in the election. This, of course, is directly contrary to the concept of primary election law (see page 111), but an astounding number of people were troubled and fooled by this argument.

In Retrospect

This is admittedly a personal account of one political campaign. It is neither all-inclusive nor objective. It is the candidate's recollection of six hectic months which climaxed eight stimulating years.

Its purpose is to give you a little of the flavor of a political campaign, and also some idea of what can be accomplished when people are willing to participate in politics. Its negative side is represented by the final vote:

Daley	708,222
Merriam	585,555

Its positive side is still being written. And it will go on for some time. As this book was being written, the *Ladies Home Journal* contained an article about a Merriam precinct worker, a housewife, entitled "Not Defeated—Just Delayed." This lady, having had a taste of political activity and of what her vote and energy can mean, has no intention of leaving it all to someone else from now on. And one of the three Democratic primary candidates in the mayoralty campaign—Adamowski—decided in 1956 to join the Republican forces, and defeated the incumbent Democratic state's attorney. His campaign was supported by the Citizens-for-Merriam group, the volunteers who cut their eyeteeth in the 1955 campaign.

Thus it is that political campaigns such as this help to awaken a sometimes complacent electorate. The moral of this story is not in the good of one side and the bad of another (because in truth the roles, politically speaking, have been reversed at different times and in different places), but rather to suggest that whatever the political conditions and whatever the party in power, you, the citizen-politician, can have something to say about your government's activities and its future —if you want to.

There are some who would say that Chicago is a horrible example of city politics. And perhaps it is. But the differences are of degree, not of kind. And the subtle transformation which slides us from the philosophy "let's just cheat a little" toward complete corruption, and possibly even tyranny, is unfortunately difficult to perceive. If government by majority is a sound philosophy, then it is never too early to begin protecting it and defending it against all threats. The history of Chicago suggests that the worst enemy of good government is neglect and lack of interest.

PART II

Citizens in Politics

CHAPTER TWO

Beginner's Guide to Practical Politics

A Frame of Reference

"All very interesting," you may say, "but what does the 1955 mayoral election in Chicago have to do with me and my problems?"

There are other than jingoistic reasons for putting this particular election under the microscope. The mayor of Chicago is one of the most important elective officials in our country; he is outranked only by the President, the mayor of New York City, and the governors of several states. Furthermore, big city government is big business: Chicago's costs more than one-half billion dollars a year. In political terms, Chicago is the long-time battleground of powerful local party organizations who thought the 1955 election important enough to spend nearly $2 million on it. The Chicago story, then, has meaning for many citizens beyond its borders.

But the real reasons for featuring this campaign lie elsewhere. First, it provides a unique opportunity to look inside an important case history of political action. Second, it serves to demonstrate the relations between the election process and the other facets of democratic government and thus illustrates strikingly the impact of party politics on the framework of government. Third—and perhaps most important—it raises in concrete terms one of the central issues of American democracy: the massive indifference of our citizens. Despite huge expenditures of money and manpower nearly one-third of Chicago's eligible citizens did not bother to vote in the election of 1955. A sample group of the nonvoters was tracked down by an opinion-polling organization and asked why. These were some of their reasons for staying home on election day:

Some did not think elections made any difference.

Some did not think their personal vote meant much.

Some did not know much about either the candidates or the offices at stake.

A few thought all public officials were crooks.

Many did not want to be bothered.

A scattering did not even believe in majority rule.

The same pattern of lack of interest appears all over the American scene. Dr. George Gallup asked a large group of mothers of American servicemen what they wanted their sons to do on their return to civilian life. One answer stood out sharply in its tragic significance. They did not want their sons to have anything to do with politics.

As a nation we have been sharply jolted by instances where citizens take their democratic responsibilities, even their loyalty, lightly. A handful of key officials in a wide range of responsible positions have admitted to passing on information to foreign powers. Several have confessed to serious disillusionment with our democratic procedures and performance. The nation was rocked when twenty-one American prisoners of the Korean War chose to stay with the Communists. Undoubtedly brainwashing had its effect, but it is increasingly clear that these men failed to understand either the democracy they chose to leave or the communism they chose to adopt. Even those who returned to the United States seemed to express more disillusionment with their Communist captors than understanding of democracy. These are the isolated extremes; but such men exhibit in exaggerated form the tragic symptoms of a serious national disorder. Their actions should be warning—if we need warning—that the time has come for every citizen to take stock.

We are being faced with the central questions of democracy: Do Americans understand that democracy depends on individual action? Do we realize that each of us must be a citizen-politician if democracy is to work? And how many of us are equipped with the knowledge and the know-how we need in order to function in present-day politics?

Other pertinent questions stem from these:

How is our political system set up to translate the wishes and the abilities of individual citizens into concerted action?

Who makes key governmental decisions? How and when and under what circumstances are these decisions made?

How can one person hope to have a hand in helping to formulate such decisions?

How are democratic leaders selected? What is the role of leadership in democracy?

Can these leaders be influenced? If so, how?

What is the role of political parties (and political independents) in elections, in governmental decision-making, in government operations at all levels?

How serious a problem is nonvoting and nonparticipation in public affairs? And what can be done about it?

The citizen-politician cannot hope to answer these questions unless he understands the forces and the institutions at work on the political scene. You would not expect to forge ahead in a business or profession without some sort of apprenticeship, and you cannot expect to be an effective citizen-politician in twentieth-century democracy without preparation and practice.

The key to your interest, and the most obvious channel for your participation, is politics—and elections. If your voice is to be heard in government you must share at least minimally in the excitement (and the disappointments) of political action. The dedicated and knowledgeable amateur citizen-politician will find, like the professional, that politics is a 365-day-a-year preoccupation. And the primary focus of this activity is the political parties.

How to Find Your Way Around in a Party

Joining a party that has no membership card

In some ways it is easy to join either of our great parties, but in other ways it is difficult. The parties are wide open in the sense that no formal barriers block the way, but practically it takes political savoir-faire to get beyond the outer fringes. There are no membership cards in the usual sense, yet the barrier between the insiders and the outsiders is real and resistant. How does one cross this invisible moat and become an insider? There are many roads, and many kinds of pass-word, but nearly all involve some sort of apprenticeship.

One obvious gateway is registration in a party primary. This will put you on your precinct committeeman's list as a "prospect." If he is alert he will come to call—at which time, if you are willing to work and/or to contribute money, "you are in." Doors will then be opened to the kind of political gossip that is invaluable in identifying the people who run your local organization. This will help you find your way around in the political activities of your area. Whatever his skills (and as in everything else there are good, bad, and indifferent workers) the precinct committeeman's experience is a first resource for the novice, and his acquaintance is a possible stepping-stone up the political ladder.

If this seems too slow, there are other approaches which you can try. At election time there will be well-publicized candidates' meetings for you to attend. Attend regularly, listen to what is said, and find out who is running them. Respond to the pleas for help (and money) and you will get on their list. It will not hurt to attend the opposition's meetings also. At least prime yourself with some knowledge of what issues they are stressing, how their candidates look, and what their support consists of. If you can appear knowledgeable, your value as a recruit immediately goes up. Nor should you overlook the meetings of the independents, if they are organized. Even a dyed-in-the-wool partisan will find their activities enlightening. There is no better place to hear unvarnished, if unflattering, truth about your party and its chances. Its weaknesses will be presented with relish, and you can pick up the kind of clues that help to fit together a political jigsaw.

Reconcile yourself to a great deal of this sort of personal sleuthing. The party's real character, strength, organization, and lines of authority are never served up to you on a silver platter. All sorts of useful information lie scattered about, but they must be pieced together with care and patience. There is much to be gleaned from the flood of publications which all political groups turn out. They are always slanted, but when the coating is peeled away the insides are juicy with facts. Political gossip columns in the daily press can be useful in discovering wheels within wheels. However, the real story of organization power and machinery is not to be found in any of these places. Perhaps it can never be fully captured in words, for its realities lie in interpersonal relationships and there is no map to these uncharted areas. Painstaking personal exploration is required. An experienced guide is invaluable but it takes a certain degree of political know-how to select such a guide.

On the political ladder: niches for volunteers

Joining a party organization by getting on the mailing lists is simple, but a better "in" is to offer to work. Political groups are always hungry for volunteers who will give a little of their time and/or money—except where the professionals have and wish to keep a tight rein on party organization. In such circumstances the citizen-politician may first have to work to dislodge the power-hungry combine before his volunteer efforts can be focused on public service. But such circumstances are now the exception rather than the rule.

Politics will greedily absorb every moment of time which its practitioners are willing to spend, but there is always a place for the volunteer whose efforts must be limited. The citizen-politician, by definition, has other interests, activities, and responsibilities, and he may have to do a little searching to find a suitable niche. But there is a happy medium between the full-time professional and the do-nothing citizen; and there are hundreds of political jobs crying out for volunteers. Here are some of the more obvious ones:

- Judges and clerks of election
- Elected party officials (from precinct committeeman to national committeeman)
- Appointed party officers (treasurer, secretary of ward or district organization, publicity officer, etc.)
- Fundraisers
- Delegates to local, state, or national conventions
- Canvassers (to check on registration of voters)
- Election day workers (runners, watchers, challengers, baby sitters, drivers, etc.)
- Campaign workers (to distribute literature, participate in telephone campaigns, work in central or local campaign office, stuff envelopes and do clerical chores, make speeches, recruit new workers, etc.)
- Leaders in civic groups who work with public officials on civic issues, organizing opposition, etc.
- And lots more.

One of the problems of politics (though it is by no means peculiar to politics) is the fact that too many people want to be generals and too few are willing to serve as working privates. Almost everyone would like to be one of the élite who make the big decisions; but there are always too few volunteers who are willing to man the precincts and do the day-today chores. Such grass roots work is not only important to the parties; it is basic political education.

In short, the quickest way to learn the art and craft of politics is to become a part of it and the best place to start is at the local level. For example, you can act as a watcher for your party in the polling place. Eleven hours of this duty will give you rich opportunities to get acquainted with your committeemen and with the election judges and clerks who are often grass roots party regulars. Also you will learn to tie together the names and faces and political leanings of your neighbors. Alongside these personal insights you will pick up much know-how concerning election law—who may vote under what circumstances, who may challenge, when, and so forth. If a voting machine is used, the job is relatively simple and quick; but with a long paper ballot it is not unusual for the judges, clerks, and watchers to work far into the night.

If you move on to become a trusted precinct worker you will be urged to attend the organization's regular political meetings. Your eligibility will be attested when you are notified of such meetings. At the ward or district level such meetings are primarily for the local workers. Here is a good place to see the organization in action: the local leader or the hometown kingpin exercises his political talents; personalities emerge, candidates and issues are silhouetted, problems and plans discussed, and enthusiasms carefully fanned. These meetings generally are informal, almost fraternal; the local organization is often called a political club. First names are tossed about and backs are slapped. The rapport that develops plays an important role in party operation. Such grass roots meetings accomplish for the local organization what the huge rallies and $100-a-plate dinners accomplish on the larger political stage. They unite the faithful, spotlight the "big brass," publicize future plans, and, most important, raise money for the party's coffers.

The small fellow soon feels like a cog in a real organization.

One quickly learns to keep an ear carefully tuned for undercover pressures, tensions, and power plays. It takes experience to detect these crosscurrents, and political astuteness develops its own kind of Geiger counter. A close study of who sits on the speakers' platform, for example, will often disclose the real as against the paper hierarchy. Such knowledge is obviously a prime political asset. Valuable light is often thrown on party activities and strategy by the reporters and political commentators who are indefatigable in ferreting out political gossip. They seldom miss noting who spoke to whom and they are quick to point out who pulls the strings on whom. Regular attention to their stories will make you familiar with key names, and more important with key relationships. And there are few more interesting pastimes. Political gossip offers a well-traveled route to the role of "the inside dopester" whom David Riesman described in *The Lonely Crowd*.[1]

Direct assaults on the stronghold of the party are only one way of accomplishing your private political objectives. Other routes, if perhaps more circuitous, are still broad and widely traveled. These weave their way through all sorts of semiofficial and auxiliary party organizations. There are many groups: the Young Democrats, the Young Republicans, student groups, women's groups, the independents, the citizens-committees-for-this-or-that, the political action groups of the trade unions, and the politically oriented wings of other powerful pressure groups. It is altogether too easy to get on their mailing lists. Once on the list you will be subjected to a steady rain of material. This deserves careful perusal, although it is generally one-sided.

It is often more difficult to stay *off* than to get on mailing lists of organizations, which leads to a word of caution. In these uneasy times it is important to remember that any

[1] David Riesman, with Nathan Glazer and Reuel Denney, *The Lonely Crowd, A Study of the Changing American Character,* abridged (New York: Doubleday and Company, 1953).

organization may be subjected to less than desirable pressures and influences. Many an earnest and unsuspecting group has been subjected to a baptism by fire of subversive elements exercising their well-practiced burrowing-from-within procedures. Many groups have had to learn through bitter experience how to recognize the fine Machiavellian hand of Moscow-directed subversion. Zealous but naïve enthusiasts have all too often awakened to the unhappy fact that they have allowed themselves to become "fellow travelers." All politically oriented organizations are natural targets for such subversion. Their ready-made structure and expertness at lobbying are valuable assets. The newcomer in politics must be on his guard, for naïveté is no match for the skill of the trained subversive. But the careful observer can sometimes turn subversive know-how to patriotic ends. The very efficiency of subversive groups provides certain lessons for the organization of democratic action.

THE ROLE OF THE PRECINCT WORKER

A successful political organization must be so structured that it can mobilize support for its candidates, its platform and—if it wins—its legislative and administrative programs. This requires effective workers, and plenty of them. To get a party's message through to voters there is no substitute for manpower—the manpower of the political foot soldier, the precinct worker in the city, and the local committeeman in other areas. There are about 150,000 precincts in the United States. They range widely in size. Rural precincts may cover many square miles, while some city skyscrapers include more than one precinct. Three or four hundred voters make up an average precint. The precincts are legal election units and precinct officials are responsible for the smooth functioning of the voting process. They help to check the accuracy of voter registration, conduct the election, and count the ballots. Precincts are always the last-ditch battlegrounds of the political parties, and party workers are valued for their ability to carry their precincts. It is a truism that elections are won or lost in these local political arenas.

Despite the growing importance of mass communication the best way to reach each and every voter is still by personal contact. There is no mechanical gadget that will get a man out of his house and to the polls. Nor can any robot argue with a recalcitrant or unconvinced voter. These are the duties of the local party workers.

In this sense, precinct workers are like the infantry—every time a weapon of destruction is invented they always say this is the end of the infantryman; but still in every war the infantry bear the brunt of the battle. So it is in politics. Every time a new communication medium is developed someone darkly prophesies the end of the precinct worker. But in every election campaign the precinct workers still bear the brunt of the work in carrying the candidate's and the party's message directly to the voters, of getting voters registered and to the polls.

Neither of the major parties has ever manned all precincts, not even in the large cities where political battles often reach white heat. In 1955 a national Republican preconvention training meeting set its sights on 200,000 additional precinct workers. In defense of the widespread practice of putting precinct workers in government jobs, it must be said that this is the surest and quickest way of recruiting party workers. If more citizen-politicians were willing to volunteer for these important legwork tasks there would be less pressure for such patronage arrangements.

There is no magic about doing precinct work: you call personally on every family in your area; you tell them whom you are working for and why you are working for him; you urge everyone to register and to vote, and you keep checking back. Both parties and assorted civic groups have published handbooks and manuals for precinct workers. An excellent one was prepared by Robert Knapp, originally for the Independent Voters of Illinois. It was called *A Precinct Manual for Citizens-for-Merriam*. Here is a sample of his advice to precinct canvassers:

EXACTLY WHAT DOES A PRECINCT CAPTAIN DO?

The work of a precinct captain can be reduced to two simple principles—and one qualification.

The Principles: 1. you *locate* your votes.
                 2. you get 'em to the polls.

The Qualification: You do it SYSTEMATICALLY.

WHAT'S THE PROFESSIONAL PRECINCT CAPTAIN GOT THAT YOU HAVEN'T?

They give full time to canvassing. They have more experience (though they had a first time, too). They have money to spend and jobs to give. They maintain a continuing relation with the voters.

WHAT HAVE YOU GOT THAT THE PRO'S DON'T HAVE?

You have convictions about what you're presenting. You have a story to tell. Many people who reject (or eject) the professional will be perfectly receptive to you. In many cases you will be able to enlist the *active* participation of many people by simply asking for help in the precinct and/or in the office. ASK for active help in the campaign.

CHECK LIST FOR CITIZENS-FOR-MERRIAM PRECINCT LEADERS REGISTRATION—30 DAYS BEFORE ELECTION

1. Canvass house to house. Learn who the new voters are. Learn who has moved away.
2. Urge new voters to register. Tell them when, where, how. Turn in removals to your local chairman.
3. The night before registration, and on registration day remind voters to register. You CAN'T remind them too often.

CANVASSING—THREE WEEKS TO ONE DAY BEFORE THE ELECTION

1. Canvass house to house. Talk to at least one member of every family. Remember your first objective is to LOCATE VOTES. In every case:

   a. Learn their attitude.
   b. Give them any information they want, or get it to them later.
   c. Give them literature.
   d. Mark your list with a plus, minus, or zero.
   e. Ask them to help you work your precinct.
2. After the full round of your precinct, go back to those doubt-
   fuls and unknowns you think you have a chance of converting.

BRINGING IN THE VOTE

1. The night before election, remind all your voters marked with
   plus.
2. Election Day, get out early; get men to vote before they leave
   for work; check all day to keep your plus marks coming to vote.
   Use every possible means to get your voters in. After the polls
   close it will be too late.

WATCHING THE COUNT

1. Be in the polls before they close. Stay for the count.
2. Watch the ballots. Watch the tally.

AT ALL TIMES—Stay busy and alert. Don't wait to be invited to
work. Keep in touch with your ward chairman. His job is to
furnish you with literature, the Precinct List, a poll watcher's
certificate. He should help you with information, guidance, counsel.
He wants your ideas and suggestions.

TIPS, CAUTIONS, QUESTIONS

TIP: *Don't be discouraged because* your precinct list looks so
     long. In a 400-voter precinct, there won't be more than 200
     households—probably less. Some households will have 6
     voters. Some will have only one. Some calls may take an
     hour. A few will take a half-hour. Most take 5 to 15 minutes.
     Some won't take 30 seconds because they won't talk or don't
     answer.

TIP: *Gauge your personal time* so you put in most work nearest
     the election, because opinions nearest election day will be
     the ones that people most likely will vote.

TIP: *Sunday afternoon* is a good time for canvassing, particularly in bad weather. Bad weather is always especially good because people admire you for going out in it.

CAUTION: *System is everything.* Don't depend just on talking to your friends. It's easier, yes—but shadow boxing is easier than fighting, too. Your friends will usually vote right anyway. It's the people you DON'T know who vote against you, mainly. You MUST get out and MEET THE PEOPLE in your precinct.

CAUTION: *Don't rely on any voter* to carry out any promise. With the best intentions in the world, ONE-THIRD of your voters will FORGET to vote.

CAUTION: Always, always do your level best to talk to the voter on election day, preferably just before he enters the polling place. He'll be impressed with your sincerity and enthusiasm and any lingering doubts will go.

Volunteers who pick up their courage and undertake to canvass a precinct nearly always find it a challenging and rewarding experience. One top television producer who enlisted in the 1955 Chicago campaign (and incidentally carried it against a professional) has recorded his satisfaction at working his precinct. Here is his story:

WORKING A PRECINCT
by Jay Sheridan

It was early March. I drew my coat collar up to shut out a raw wind that whipped pieces of paper down the streets. I checked my watch . . . 7:32 P.M. . . . I had to hurry. "How did I ever get into this anyhow? . . . I'm a television producer, happy with my work, and doing very well, now suddenly I'm in *this*, how did it happen?" I shook my head as I tried to answer myself. This was the moment I had feared. There it stood, the large and foreboding house I had to get into. . . . 7:40 P.M. . . . no time to waste. I muttered, "Okay, Sheridan, let's go." As I slowly climbed the steps I noticed no lights in the front room. . . . Maybe no one's home . . . maybe I should try tomorrow . . . "Come on, Sheridan, cut it out, ring that bell." . . . The bell sounded tremendously loud as it shattered the stillness . . . wait . . . wait . . . wait. Now footsteps coming! This is it! Control yourself! You know what you have to do! But you've never done it before!

The door opened. He was a man about forty. . . . Shorter than you are, Sheridan. You know his name . . . you even know his politics. You've rehearsed this a hundred times. Now do it!

"Mr. Stone?"

"Yes."

There was a rush of words. "My name is Jay Sheridan, I live down on the next block and I'm canvassing our precinct for the Citizens-for-Merriam."

"Oh yes, won't you come in."

I had made it, I was in the house. The Stones knew and liked Merriam. They were registered Republicans. Mr. Stone was a precinct captain once himself. They were following the campaign closely and agreed completely with the way you felt about Bob Merriam and Chicago politics.

"Will you have a glass of beer, Mr. Sheridan?"

"No, thanks, I have a lot of calls to make." You check your precinct list. "How about Mr. and Mrs. Greenhut who are registered at this address?" They're Mrs. Stone's parents and both for Merriam. They are for my man! Four votes! You'll have to be sure to get this family out on election day!

I hardly felt the front steps as I left. This job was easy and fun. Now I knew why I was doing this. This is where elections are won, in the precincts, and it was so easy. I bounced up to the next house and jauntily rang the bell. Footsteps again . . . good . . . the door opened a crack and I could tell the latch was still on.

"Who's there!" said a chilly voice.

"Mrs. Shire?"

"Yes."

"I'm Jay Sheridan, I live in the next block and I'm canvassing our precinct for the Citizens-for-Merriam."

"Listen, you, I happen to know that all you politicians are crooks, and I don't want any ward heelers coming around bothering us. It won't do you no good anyway because my husband and me don't vote. Both sides are crooks and we don't believe in crooks!" The door slammed in my face.

As I walked down the steps I wondered again, "How the hell did I ever get into this?" I thought a moment and then I knew. I had to go back three months to answer my own question. The mayoralty campaign was just starting. The Republican candidate was Robert E. Merriam. I had produced some television programs for him the year before and had great admiration for him as a public servant. At the start of his campaign he had asked if I would be interested in producing his TV programs. I said, "Certainly I would be," and that's how it all started. That's all it was to me, just a job. I sat in on the many script meetings and started turning out the program. Naturally I became familiar with the issues concerned. I saw an awful lot of things about my city government that I didn't like. I became convinced that Mr. Merriam could and would do something about them. It was no longer just a job, I was going to help Chicago become a better city in which to live. I was at campaign headquarters all the time as the television campaign stepped up. I was in on top level meetings concerning the problems and conduct of the campaign. It was very exciting to a political neophyte like me.

Then came primary night. Though our "Tiger" (see how professional I was getting? That term for a candidate fascinated me) was uncontested, the primary vote was disappointing. What had happened? What had gone wrong? Headquarters buzzed.

"You can't expect a big primary vote when your man is uncontested!"

"The bitter fight in the Democratic primary took the show away from us!"

"It threatened rain; everybody stayed home."

The door of the inner office opened and Irv Koppel, one of the best precinct captains in the city, walked in.

"What happened, Irv, what happened?"

"My precinct came in 5 to 1 for us with a 78 per cent turnout."

"Yes, Irv, but you're an old hand, you're a good man in the precinct. What happened in the rest of the city?"

"We've got too damn many generals, not enough privates!"

The statement hit me like a sledgehammer. I had been an enlisted man during the war. I had the Purple Heart. I knew the generals were important but I don't think you ever get over the fierce feeling that privates win the battles. Ask any private! And here I'd been sitting in headquarters like a general. This campaign was very important to my city, and I had great faith that my candidate would make the finest mayor our city had ever had. And what was I doing? Being a general at headquarters! At that moment I decided to become a "private" in "combat" in my precinct. I had no idea where to start so I got a pamphlet called *A Precinct Manual for Citizens-for-Merriam* by Robert Knapp. This pamphlet is certainly the biggest help that any newcomer to precinct work could have. "So that is it, Sheridan, that is why you started out tonight, why you got into this . . . now stop standing here . . . forget about that woman and get up to the next house. It can't be any worse than the last one . . . This is 'combat,' remember? . . ."

The next family was very pleasant but undecided.

"Yes, we think Merriam is the best man, but we're Democrats."

"So am I."

"Aren't you the Republican precinct captain?"

"No, the Citizens-for-Merriam is an independent group. We have thousands of Democrats working for us."

"Oh, I didn't know that. But what could Merriam do?"

"Look what he did as an alderman. There he was only one out of fifty! Just think what strides he could make for the city as mayor!"

And so it went. Questions from two intelligent people who were anxious to make the right decision. I left literature and promised to check with them again, and once more I knew why I had decided to work my precinct.

By the time I had finished canvassing the whole precinct I knew that it was one of the most rewarding experiences of my life. I had some rebuffs like my second house but very few. Most people were very interested in the election, whether they were for your man or not. One of my major fears, that I didn't know enough about the election to answer questions intelligently, was completely unfounded. I have decided that by the time you are interested enough in an election to work a precinct you probably know more about the issues and the candidates than 95% of the people you talk to.

Election Day! Up at five o'clock to be a poll watcher. I can't express my feelings as I watched *my* voters coming to the polling place.

"Good morning, Mr. Lewellen" . . . he's against . . . never voted against his party in his life and he isn't going to start now. . . .

"Good morning, Mr. Kammert" . . . that's one for us . . . even told me he had converted some of his friends to our side. . . .

"Good morning, Mrs. Stone" . . . remember? . . . your first house . . . she's on our side. . . .

"Good morning, Mr. Knox" . . . he had been undecided . . . I hope the literature I left did some good. . . .

Afternoon . . . 3:00 P.M. . . . check the registration list . . . which voters who were for your man haven't voted yet . . . go to their houses . . . "I'll be happy to baby sit while you run over and vote." . . . "I'd be happy to drive your grandmother if it's too far to walk." . . . a good turnout today . . . I wonder how it's going. . . .

5:00 P.M. . . . The polls close . . . how did we do? . . . How did we do? . . . Get that voting machine open. . . . Let's see . . . let's see. . . . Merriam 259 . . . Daley 84 ! ! ! we DID IT! . . . I had carried *my* precinct by better than three to one! . . . *my* precinct had never done that before! . . . Jay Sheridan had influenced the election in his own precinct in the 8th ward in the City of Chicago, in the County of Cook. I had never felt so close to my neighborhood and my community before. . . . It's a feeling hard to describe, but the realization that I had actually influenced the voting in *my* precinct gave me a sense of satisfaction that I have never experienced before.

Into the car and down to headquarters with the good news. Began to get the reports on the radio . . . not good . . . the opposition leads . . . at headquarters . . . the over-all picture is very bad . . . 12:00 midnight . . . time to concede . . . a bitter moment . . . all that work . . . what happened? . . . what went wrong? Get another cup of coffee . . . you've had nine, one more won't hurt. . . . What happened? . . . You don't know the answer. *Could it be that too many citizens felt they wouldn't make good privates because they're not "pros"?* . . . stir your coffee . . . you wonder . . . *could it possibly be that we had too many*

generals and not enough privates? . . . Stir your coffee . . . stir
your coffee . . . and wonder.

Volunteer political workers, particularly in impersonal
urban communities, often feel themselves at a disadvantage
against those professionals whose patronage job makes it
possible for them to work their precincts intensively and who
may even have favors to pass out. But the activities of the two
sorts of workers (as long as the patronage worker operates
legally) are much the same. The difference, where it exists,
boils down to service and availability—often twenty-four hours
a day and 365 days a year. The volunteer can learn nearly
everything he needs to know—except invaluable first-hand
interviewing experience—from observing the professional in
action.

At its best the precinct captain-constituent relationship is a
personal one, with friendly feelings interlarded with more
practical considerations. Pronouncements of candidates on
issues may influence some votes but the local party worker
does not comfortably rest on such supports. He cultivates an
intimate relationship with his constituents. He is the neighbor
who may become a friend in need. Wherever possible, he does
his constituents favors in full expectation that they will vote
for his man.

In the old days the precinct committeeman was a kind of
glorified social worker to whom one could turn in times of
trouble. If you had little or no money and were at the mercy
of a great impersonal city, or fell victim to some catastrophe,
"good old precinct-captain Joe" knew what to do. He could
get you on relief. He could help you out with the police when
your kid was in trouble. He'd help get your sick wife to the
hospital. He'd tell you who to see at the city hall. He might
even be able to get "big shots" to find you a city job when you
were down on your luck.

And how and why could Joe do all these things? Joe had the

connections which made these services possible. Of course in return he expected you to vote for his man. And he counted on your grateful family and a lot of your friends to do like-wise. The word got around that Joe was a good man to know. It was only natural that some of his virtues would rub off on his candidate, and you would be anxious to let him know that you had voted "regular." Even when you did not need any-thing from Joe, it made you feel good to know that he took an interest in you and your family. Who wouldn't like the person who remembered that your boy Tom had broken a leg, or that your wife had just had a new baby? And who wouldn't relish getting a political tip from Joe at the local tavern? Joe was a nice friendly sort of fellow with no airs, probably even went to your own church. And he was not above gilding his own glamour with a bit of calculated name-dropping and political gossip. It was nice to know a fellow who knew all the higher-ups. You never knew when that might come in handy. This was Joe—the precinct captain. His name was legion, and although such old style Joe's are gradually disappearing, they are by no means extinct.

Some Joes are part of a boss-ridden machine, in which case they take orders, and sometimes have illegal favors to work with. They can engineer a simple "fix," and have dollars to hand out for "expenses" on election day. They might even be able to guarantee that nothing would happen if a tavern stayed open after legal closing hours or served beer to minors. And if a little card game was going on in the back room, "nobody would say nothing." In his small way the machine precinct captain becomes a local "big shot." The fact that he might be involved in a tie-up between a big-time crime syn-dicate and politics may or may not be apparent. And there is always the chance to rationalize his actions as not hurting any-body, or as necessary to keep the right people in office.

The amateur citizen-politician can and does successfully compete with the professionals when the game is aboveboard, but the job differs greatly in different neighborhoods. Lower-income families and immigrants have greater need for service and therefore are more susceptible to the advice of the local party worker; higher-income families and the native-born are better able to shift for themselves. To the southern rural Negroes who are flocking to the northern cities, the social services function of the precinct captain—and his personal recommendation—are still tremendously important. This fact showed up in the Chicago campaign. An opinion poller met this story. A young woman, fresh from the South, said she voted straight Democratic. She said this was her first voting experience. Asked how she happened to vote as she did, she replied, "I just went around looking for the precinct captain, and asked him how to vote."

The main weakness of amateur party workers is that they are prone to treat the job as a one-month—election month—assignment. No professional takes so shortsighted a view. He knows that he is most persuasive if he is no stranger when he comes to call. When it comes to many county or local offices, a good precinct committeeman can often claim with truth that the voter was really voting for him rather than for the candidate. What he means is that the voter who does not have much interest in a particular candidate will sometimes vote on the basis of friendship with the precinct worker. Thus the precinct committeeman who is on the job around the calendar can "deliver" as no Johnny-come-lately can hope to.

The citizen-politician can make a major contribution—and enjoy being in the thick of political things—if he will offer his services to do precinct work. He does not have to take on the whole job of precinct committeeman. He can help with any part of it, canvassing, distributing literature, posters, and campaign buttons, poll watching, even judging elections. And most important, he can talk about the election and its issues with his acquaintances.

When responsible and interested citizens participate in election activities their example is far more persuasive than any amount of exhortation. There is much evidence that the example of a respected person is the strongest force for pushing citizen inertia off dead center. The Science Research Associates polls (described in detail in Chapter Seven) suggest that while most people talk about the importance of voting, they fail to make the effort unless they are strongly motivated. (The Great Depression was the kind of traumatic national experience that pushed millions of previously lackadaisical voters into the polling places.) These studies also make it clear that politically active persons generally had politically active parents. Therefore, if you want your children to be citizen-politicians you had better be one yourself!

Your reward will also be immediate and personal. Anyone who has canvassed his own neighborhood to get potential voters registered will have the agreeable experience of being received with respect, as one who is doing a civic job out of which he personally gets nothing but satisfaction. There are many other ways of making one's political weight felt, but as Jay Sheridan pointed out, there are few more satisfying ones.

The precinct committeeman and his helpers are, and will continue to be, the backbone of the party—the infantrymen of politics. And any citizen-politician can make a rewarding contribution at this level. He can have no better initiation into party activity. Moreover every increase in the numbers of active citizen-politicians strengthens the parties and undercuts the influence of patronage-fed precinct workers.

CHAPTER THREE

Citizen Action and the Two-Party System

PARTIES AND POPULAR CONSENT

The business of government in a democracy is everybody's business, but it is not the sort of business that everybody can conduct on his own. Without amplification, few voices are strong enough to be heard; without reinforcement, individual human strength is always too slight. It takes great gifts to be able to emerge from the anonymity of the crowd, but in organization there is telling strength for everyone and the cumulative power of the crowd can make itself forcibly felt. The scope and nature of government decisions, in contrast to those of other groups, involve everyone, and this fact still further dwarfs the individual. All of which makes it doubly important for him to join forces with others in the same situation. It should already be clear that, generally speaking, politics means parties.

The official-unofficial status of the political parties

Political parties are not mentioned anywhere in the Constitution of the United States, yet their existence bulwarks the entire system of American government. Our two-party system is an essential device for organizing the collective will of our democracy. There is no "official" party in the United States as there was in Nazi Germany and is now in the Soviet Union. In these dictatorships minority parties are a kind of window-dressing, while the official parties really run the country. At best citizens are allowed the "privilege" of voting *Yes* when such endorsement suits the purposes of their rules; a *No* vote generally entails serious personal hazards. In America the political party is the instrument of citizens, not the tool of an entrenched oligarchy. Party orthodoxy—when it is achieved—has to be built from within.

The American political parties although unofficial and extra-constitutional operate at every level of government. They are recognized somewhat obliquely since they are regulated by law, and election procedures are often rigorously supervised. Their activities even have a measure of public subsidy. Ballots are printed, voting machines are supplied, election records are maintained, and clerks and judges of election are paid fees from the public coffers. Although legislative restrictions— many of them designed to safeguard the citizen's right to work through the party of his choice—have expanded, the internal affairs of the parties are still largely a private matter.

The free-swinging independence of American political parties—their usefulness in organizing the consent of the governed —depends on the very personal right of being able to choose and to work in the party of one's choice. Freedom of conscience, of expression, and of assembly are essential. The vigorous growth of these freedoms is indeed reflected in the strength of America's two-party system. No other system has yet proved itself so capable of expressing the free choices of so many people, and this success is fed by the dynamism of the Bill of Rights.

Political parties exercise powerful influence at every level and in every phase of governmental operation. Each party struggles to get and to hold the reins of political power and therefore concerns itself with the executive and the judicial as well as the legislative branches of government. They naturally have a single-minded approach to segmented government. In trying to draw tight the reins of control they force a kind of teamwork on all three branches of government and goad each other into political invention from which the public profits.

Political parties also play an important role in helping to tie together our national-state-local government system. They act as watchdogs on operations at all levels. Altogether American government functions through some 100,000 different units: national, local, and state. Thanks to these numbers of governments neither party can ever tightly control all levels of government, and this fact in itself provides safeguards against abusive rule by a temporary majority. It also keeps the game of politics at a lively pitch.

The political parties play their continuing and essential part in every facet of American government. They represent the organized interest of citizens as citizens and are the main, the most direct, although not the exclusive channel, for effective citizen action. Thus government "of the people, by the people, for the people" is in one sense government by political party.

Party organization: a loose-jointed pyramid

American parties are loosely organized from the ground up, with some few strands running from the top down. The pyramidal structure shown in Fig. 1 is rather neater than the reality which it tries to represent. The connections between the various levels are neither as tight nor as direct as such a diagram would indicate. The pyramid is simply a rationalization after the fact that serves to highlight the logical elements in party organization. Parties are far from completely logical, and in the course of their Topsy-like growth a variety of ways of relating the different levels of organization have been improvised. The party committeemen at every level are selected according to party rules except where these have

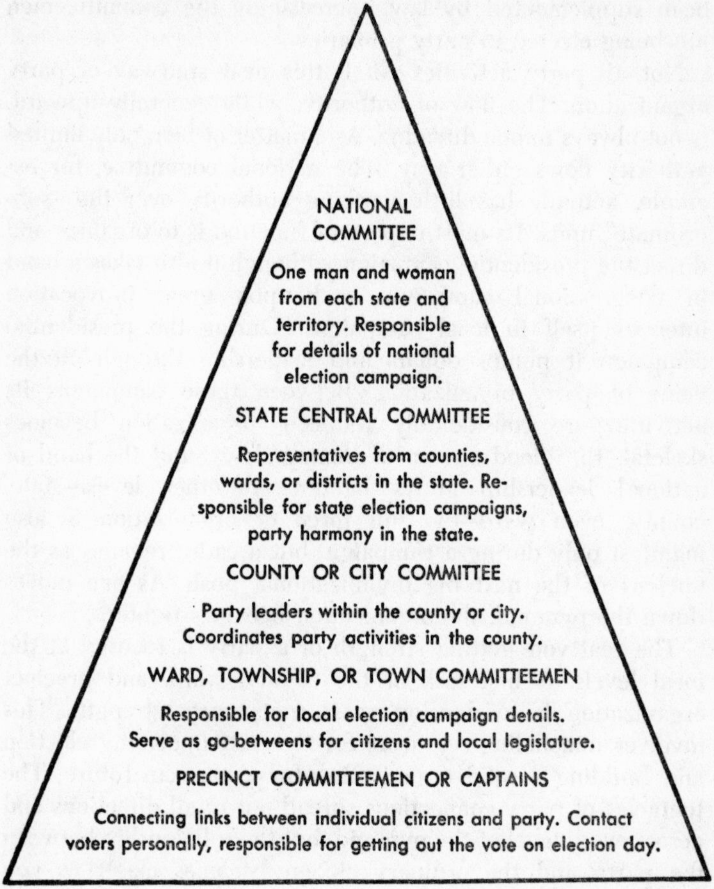

NATIONAL COMMITTEE

One man and woman from each state and territory. Responsible for details of national election campaign.

STATE CENTRAL COMMITTEE

Representatives from counties, wards, or districts in the state. Responsible for state election campaigns, party harmony in the state.

COUNTY OR CITY COMMITTEE

Party leaders within the county or city. Coordinates party activities in the county.

WARD, TOWNSHIP, OR TOWN COMMITTEEMEN

Responsible for local election campaign details. Serve as go-betweens for citizens and local legislature.

PRECINCT COMMITTEEMEN OR CAPTAINS

Connecting links between individual citizens and party. Contact voters personally, responsible for getting out the vote on election day.

Fig. 1. The Party Hierarchy—a Loose Structure

been supplemented by law. Increasingly the committeemen are being elected in party primaries.

Not all party activities climb this neat stairway of party organization. The flow of authority, while generally upward, is not always in one direction. As a matter of fact, only limited authority flows either way. The national committee, for example, actually has little working authority over the "subordinate" units. Its most important function is to organize and direct the presidential campaign, although it also takes a hand in congressional campaigns and upon great provocation interests itself in local campaigns. During the presidential campaign it pumps dollars and leadership through all the veins of party organization. Between these campaigns its activities are considerably reduced, organization becomes skeletal, the blood stream of money slows, and the hand of national leadership grows lighter. At other levels—state, county, even ward—the full force of organization is also manifest only during a campaign, but a cadre remains as the nucleus of the next big organizational push. As one moves down the pyramid, the organization becomes tighter.

The real vote-getting strength of a party is focused at the local levels. A first task of the county, ward, and precinct organization is to develop grass roots party strength. This involves marshaling resources for the next upcoming election and building a solid organization for a partisan future. The tentacles of party connections spread out in all directions and across every level of the pyramid, but the relationship between the party and the ordinary citizen becomes closer as you descend the organizational scale. The party always makes its strongest appeal to everyday citizens in face-to-face contacts. It campaigns for their confidence, votes, and support by beating party drums and by implied promises to deliver good government.

The party is not only a vote-getting organization; it also serves as a bridge between the citizen and his government. It carries citizen wishes, needs, and demands to legislators, administrators, and party functionaries—and it carries public understanding the other way. Such party know-how helps grease the machinery of democratic government and smooths the path to the sources of government services. Party officials are specialists in this—it is their stock in trade. Their know-how serves decent citizens (and sometimes grafters) and is important at every level of government. Parties teach citizens what they may expect from their government and how to go about getting what they deserve or what they want. They also provide guide services through the mazes of popular government.

These services are so valuable that they are an ever-present temptation to illegitimate operators. Party know-how can command a high price and unhappily is sometimes bought and sold for all sorts of quids-pro-quo (as we shall see later). Even legitimate favors like no-parking permits, zoning exemptions, and so forth, under some circumstances become illegitimate if they are bought and sold. But the fact that favors can be pushed over the borderline of legitimacy does not deny the civic importance of the party's bridgelike role.

The party's network of public and private services depends on closely maintained contacts both with government personnel and with private citizens. These contacts naturally are most numerous at the local level but they exist at every level and even crossweave vertically and diagonally between levels. Lines of influence build many patterns and take on all shades of firmness. Thus the local committeeman inevitably has contacts with local officials such as aldermen, commissioners, county committeemen, ward superintendents, and so forth. Similarly state central committeemen will have close and continuous working arrangements with the state officials whose fortunes they have helped to mold. Across the line that divides the legal from the illegal favor, the connections are less obvious and the most important ones never appear on paper. But a knowing politician is able to draw his own mental chart of party-government relationships, complete with lines of influence. Some of these lines can be sharply and broadly drawn but others are written in a kind of invisible ink, decipherable only by the initiate. Such realistic charting is an invaluable political asset.

The pyramidal pattern of party organization is not neatly blanketed across the whole of the nation. The party system, like the government itself, is federated not integrated. In our system of government the sovereign states delegate limited power *up* to the national government and *down* to the local county, city, and township governments. Residual authority rests in the states—and this is also where most regulation of partisan activities takes place. State party organizations are as various as the forty-eight states themselves, and any political jurisdiction is likely to be a kind of law unto itself. Party business is also variously subject to state law. State authority over such matters stems from the fact that voting rights and regulations are reserved to the sovereign states rather than the national government, except as spelled out in the Constitution.

The structure of the parties has come about largely as a by-product of their own growth processes. In the American scheme of things, parties are associations of free citizens who come together to effect the functioning of government, and despite increasing regulation remain *private, voluntary,* self-governing organizations. The national committees are not under the jurisdiction of any one state, and most of their activities are not the sort to which the delegated powers of the national government apply. Even the Republican and Democratic congressional committees are extra-legal.

In recent years the Congress has become increasingly concerned with partisan activities. It has undertaken to limit political activities of national government employees through the Hatch Acts. These forbid party fund solicitation of public employees and put limits on other sorts of political activities of public employees. Their purpose is to prevent party members from exercising undue influence on public servants. However, national conventions and the operations of the national committees are subject to little or no legislation. They remain the responsibilities of their own membership and its leadership.

An interesting example of the looseness of party organization was provided by the Democratic party following their 1956 presidential defeat. The "outs" in politics always are faced with the problem of where leadership lies. Traditionally the defeated presidential candidate is the titular head of the party, but actually the party's record is made to a great extent by its action in Congress. The Chairman of the Democratic National Committee conceived the idea of forming an advisory council including Presidential candidate Stevenson, former President Truman, key congressional leaders, and others, who were to set an off-year course of action for the Democratic party, and presumably to advise on congressional strategy. The Democratic congressional leaders refused to serve on the advisory committee, indicating that they would develop their own strategy and policies without interference from the Democratic National Committee or its new advisory group.

Public functions of political parties

Parties are many-faceted, but their activities can loosely be classified thus:

1. Activities re government
2. Activities re the party itself
3. Activities re citizens

The first of these inevitably takes top priority. A party, if it is to stay alive, needs at least reasonable hope of success in its bid for the reins of government. If its supporters lose hope the organization rapidly becomes impotent. This has been the fate of most third-party movements in the United States. It takes organization, patience, resources, and ingenuity—even luck—to get and hold the reins of political power. The processes of administering a party with millions of members and many more millions of contacts is extremely complicated. It is, indeed, big business—and its various facets are treated at some length in the following chapters.

The parties perform functions which go well beyond their own self-interest, for *they organize and channel citizen participation in government.* This role is so important to democratic government that political scientists are fond of pointing out that if parties did not exist they would have to be invented. They crystallize sentiment and work out the means of making it effective; they provide the leadership and the machinery that keep the majority moving toward a consensus; and they have the final responsibility—in power and out—of protecting the rights of the minorities.

Specifically, the parties perform the following public services:

1. Focus public issues and formulate government policy
2. Select key public officials
3. Guide government administration (or act as its critic)
4. Educate public servants and citizens
5. Act as intermediaries between citizens and government (maintaining continuity, settling differences, providing two-way communication)

Each of these roles is of supreme importance to the democratic process, and together they can make or break it.

What parties are and are not

There is nothing mysterious about parties; they are simply organized ways of getting things done. Any political organization functions in terms of some clearly felt drive. The combination of deeply held purpose and efficient structure can make a powerful team, and any party always hopes it can become a steam roller carrying the party toward political control.

Parties are built around cores of self-interest; some of these involve such things as jobs, favors, and party loyalty, but issues of public policy are always important foci. America's two great political parties have achieved notable longevity because they are flexible alignments of a variety of interests and groups. These alignments may be different in varying political arenas and under different circumstances. For example, areas of difference at the national level do not always have equivalent meaning at the state and local levels. Thus the Democrats in the past have traditionally favored lower tariffs than the Republicans, a difference which could be important in the campaigns for Congress and the Senate but has little meaning in most local contests (unless it can be translated into a "pro or con business" attitude). National party planks on such matters as labor problems or social legislation are more readily transferable to state capitols. And there are some issues, such as civil rights, that are compelling even at city hall.

Both political parties are loose and changing federations of special interests—whether or not their members are aware of this fact. People tend to join with other people who are on their side; thus the major binding adhesive of the parties is self-interest—actual or fancied. The party alignment may be on ideological grounds. In every election there are likely to be hotly contended issues. The Democratic Party, for example, made much of the New Deal and the Fair Deal, and the Republicans currently talk about modern Republicanism. But ideological frameworks are only part of the story, for political loyalties have other bases as well. Traditions and attitudes also make strong political cement. Sometimes this cement is bonded by promises of gain—power, influence, contracts, jobs, or special privileges. Such things are powerful magnets. Both parties are quick to try to capitalize on the popularity of particular issues: liberty, national defense, prosperity, and so forth. But party platforms may fail to draw hard and fast ideological lines; they often lack structured consistency. Nevertheless, lines are always drawn between the parties.

Most citizens think of themselves as either Democrats or Republicans; many are dyed-in-the-wool partisans, and a good share of the rest have partisan leanings. Such political predilections prevail unless some specific issue or some candidate has strong enough appeal to shift the balance. The importance of party allegiance was clearly demonstrated in the Chicago election.

Why people vote as they do is not always clear. Voting behavior provides fascinating material for the political scientist and the psychologist. However any listing of factors that support party allegiance will include such matters as family tradition, occupation, economic or social status, education, national background, religious affiliation, geographic location, and urban or rural background. Even though we are a young nation we tend to become mired down in political habits. Thus until recently New England was known as a rock-ribbed Republican stronghold, and the South was solidly Democratic (the 1952 and 1956 swings of certain southern states to President Eisenhower have made political history).

Class distinctions are reputedly woven into the phenomenon of party loyalty. The Republican Party has been identified in many minds with the moneyed business element, with suburbia, with the relatively conservative Northeast and the prosperous farmers. The Democrats, on the other hand, popularly have been identified with crowded city dwellers, the foreign born and other minorities, the trade unionists, and the tenant farmers. But members of all these groups are found in both parties. In any given contest economic status, occupation, geography, or any other factor may be outweighed by policy issues, although bred-in-the-bone loyalty is hard to shake. No one factor is ever controlling; the differences are in quantity rather than in kind. And there are wider differences within the parties than between them. Despite the fact that such issues as "liberal *vs.* conservative" repeatedly crop up, such terms are usually so loosely used as to be almost meaningless. The citizen-politician owes it to himself to do more than a little soul searching on the subject of his own party loyalty and its meaning in the realities of his total situation.[1]

Our federal system of government profoundly affects both our party structure and its operation. Decentralized government has brought about decentralized parties; and state, local, and regional party groupings are often strongly independent. Republicans on the two coasts do not always see eye-to-eye with those in the land-locked Middle West. The northern and southern factions of the Democratic Party have differed widely on such questions as the disposition of tidelands oil, regulation of natural gas production, states' rights, and civil rights. In the 1948 presidential convention a strong civil rights platform engineered by the northern Democrats precipitated a walkout of some southern delegations and the formation of a Dixiecrat wing that pushed J. Strom Thurmond for President. Similar fissures carried over to 1952 when some Southerners bolted the party and supported General Eisenhower. They were a central feature of the Democratic convention again in 1956. But heated controversy is not peculiar to the Democrats; the Eisenhower and Taft forces in the Republican convention in 1952 fought bitterly. And some Republicans in Congress still balk at parts of President Eisenhower's legislative program.

Policy lines are still harder to draw in local politics. In Chicago many Democratic aldermen gave only lip service to such matters as public housing and rent control, which had strong national Democratic support. The Republican aldermen

[1] If this discussion of party preferences and party alignment seems a bit cautious, it is! The authors, being on opposite sides of the political fence, have had to stick to those areas in which they could agree. Obviously they could not agree on their evaluations of the virtues and vices of the parties. However, they do agree emphatically on the importance of a party's standing for something, and on the responsibility of each citizen-politician to help his own party make its standard one to which he can rally with pride and loyalty.

proved to be more "liberal" in these matters although Republican leadership in Congress had tended to be more "conservative."

Although the policy line may be shadowed, the party label always exerts enormous pulling power. Opinion polls taken by the Merriam organization clearly demonstrated this political power. In the 1955 mayoral election their candidate's pulling power took a sharp dive between October and January, *after* he made an announcement that he would run in the Republican primary.

	All Respondents		Democrats	
	Oct. 1–10	Jan. 15–16	Oct. 1–10	Jan. 15–16
No preference	29%	24%	23%	19%
Preference	71	76	77	81
Merriam	27	19	23	8
Daley	4	15	5	24
Kennelly	26	37	33	42
Adamowski	12	6	13	6

Thus with no change in platform or in philosophy, Merriam immediately became a less popular candidate under the Republican label than he had been as a straight Independent.

Each party has a life-and-death stake in closing up the ideological and other fissures that keep breaking open in its own organization. The strangest of political bedfellows keep turning up, for political power is attractive bait. The high art of creative compromise is nowhere more greatly needed than in party politics, for a sell-out can sell all of us dangerously short.

The knowledgeable citizen will see parties as important political functionaries, but also as antagonists in a grim fight for survival. All sorts of weapons, even illegal ones, are sometimes employed; and none is more potent than party symbols. These symbols have great influence because they concentrate meanings and invest them with strong emotional overtones. Emotionally-tuned attitudes and loyalties are triggers to human action, and when they are in good working order rational arguments can have hard sledding. We all know how smoothly reason slides off the well-greased back of entrenched prejudices. The emotional weight attaching to party symbols always gives the opposition a difficult time. The parties themselves have become arch-symbols, and around the donkey and the elephant are ranged armies of lesser party symbols. Slogans bristling with emotion are a time-honored form of verbal symbolism. They are especially useful in heaping abuse on the opposition while trying to touch one's own party with angels' wings. Rallies, propaganda, and entire campaigns are carefully engineered with full reliance on the power of symbols to help hold the parties together. Whatever else they may be, the parties are systems of loyalties, and tightening these loyalties is always a primary concern.

The fluidity of the political scene provides forecasters with an endless variety of changing variables and explains why major political contests are so unpredictable. Who can foresee how a person inside the polling booth will decide in that last split second before making his mark or pulling the lever? A morning newscast can unsettle a delicate balance of opinion, or the sight of a precinct captain's face can firm a resolve. How can any voter weigh the pressures that bombard him? How is any prognosticator to read these hidden signs? It is small wonder that political pollsters have such an unhappy time of it. No matter how scientific their methods, their calculations can always be upset in the time lapse between pulse counting and election day. President Truman's election in 1948 is the classic case of such an upset.

In attaining maturity both parties have had to adapt themselves to profound changes; they have had to develop a kind of living, protoplasmic quality. Each is a growing coral reef of political activity, building out tenuously from a compact and solid center. The growth occurs on the vast outer edge of the amorphous political mass. Both parties persistently send out tentacles into new territories, seeking new sources of strength; both have to be loose, ill-defined federations if they are to become the political homes of great and diverse segments of the electorate. Sometimes all that is constant is a nucleus that may be all but unfathomable. But there is always present the ambition to hold the reins of government. This ambition acts like a gyroscope which helps the parties ride out shifting political winds.

Both parties, in adapting themselves to the exigencies of the rapidly changing national picture, have had to become common-denominators-in-flux. But they still remain as they began—clusters of interests built around the kind of give-and-take that is the price of political power. This is not to say that the ideal of public service is lacking, for political parties are no more selfish than any other human organization. Indeed, dedicated public service is their stock in trade. In the long run the public interest is their interest, although in the short run anything can happen. If they have been capable of all sorts of skulduggery they have also been able to rise to great challenges. They are the training ground of statesmen and the breeding ground of political inventiveness. It would be hard to persuade Americans that there is a better way of keeping government responsive to the people.

Whatever their public service, parties are competing institutions. They are always engaged in a fight for survival. The opposition party always wants the jobs, the prestige, and the power; and frequently there are those within the party who think they can run it better than its present leaders. Termites of ambition keep nibbling at each organization's vitals, and factions are quick to coalesce around differences. The business of building up and tearing down alignments goes on continuously.

But despite the haziness of their boundaries, our major parties are firmly rooted foci of political preferences. Parties appeared early in our national history, although they did not enter into the calculations of the Founding Fathers. Alexander Hamilton unwittingly helped to launch them when he rallied support for a strong national government. His views were stoutly opposed by the anti-federalists, and two parties were born of this historic cleavage. One of these, the Federalists, gave way before the National Republicans in the first quarter of the nineteenth century. The National Republicans became the Whigs in 1834, who in turn became the Republicans under the leadership of Abraham Lincoln. The anti-federalists gave way before the Jacksonian Democratic-Republicans, who soon were renamed the Democrats. Ever since the Civil War, Republicans and Democrats have held the center of the political stage, needled occasionally by the abortive bids of third parties. During all this time their strength has been so evenly balanced that the contest between them has remained vital; neither has held the reins of national government for longer than a score of years.

Measuring party strength

The dimensions of the parties defy precise measurement; we are not a nation of party card carriers and the census asks no questions about political party affiliation. Party strength, in so far as it can be measured, must be approximated. Party records are generally private property and would be less than conclusive even if available. The loosely jointed party structure paralleling government levels makes measurement still harder. Votes cast in party primaries come closest to being official figures but not all jurisdictions have primaries, and such elections are notoriously ill-attended. Information on campaign contributions, where available, throws important light on party strength, but again not all jurisdictions require that these figures be reported.

The contest for the presidency brings out the largest number of voters, but it often coaxes out little more than half of the potential vote. In 1952 the turnout was higher than usual; some 61,250,000 votes out of a possible total of approximately 100 million were cast. President Eisenhower received a plurality of some 7 million votes. In the midterm election of 1954—in the best midterm tradition—the tables were turned in favor of the Democrats but only 40,354,000 votes were cast. The 1956 vote was the largest yet cast, totaling approximately 62 million, but in terms of percentage of eligible adults it probably was slightly smaller than the 1952 vote. This time President Eisenhower received a plurality of over 9.5 million votes.

Statistics would indicate that the American voting record is a sorry contrast to that of other democratic countries; England, France and Italy often turn out as high as 85 per cent of the eligible voters. However, there are some extenuating circumstances: ours is a shifting population, and various state residence requirements result in considerable disbarment; the turnout tends to be smaller in one-party states, particularly in the South, where the poll-tax and other restrictions contribute to the disfranchisement of a large number of potential voters; and we do not follow the tradition in some countries of declaring a national holiday on election day or of holding the election on Sunday, as they do in France. But these circumstances still only partially explain our voting habits, or lack of them.

The importance of the so-called independent vote is hard to assess. Most independents are belligerent and articulate voters, not nonvoters; and generally they have party leanings. There are some voters who are independent on principle, and there are undoubtedly many others who feel little or no commitment to either party, but most if forced to choose would say, "I usually vote Democrat [or Republican]."

Actually party and independent strength both elude the political statistician. Not even Univac has been able to tie these factors down to precise dimensions. Active workers are perhaps the best measure of party strength; but here again we must rely on approximations. A Gallup poll estimated that 3,020,000 Democrats and 2,160,000 Republicans worked in the 1954 congressional campaigns. Two out of three of these volunteers were men, and there were nearly twice as many persons over fifty as under thirty years of age. The same poll estimated that an additional 16.4 million men and women would like to do volunteer work for the parties. This latter figure breaks down as follows:

| | *Estimated Would-be Party Workers* | |
	Democrats	*Republicans*
Men	5,200,000	3,100,000
Women	4,600,000	3,500,000
Total	9,800,000	6,600,000

If these would-be workers are added to the reported actual workers, the grand total of potential party workers reaches the impressive figure of 21,580,000. This total is made up of 8,760,000 Republicans and 12,820,000 Democrats. It is important to stress the fact that these are *potential* workers. These figures clearly do not indicate the relative strength of the two parties; otherwise we would not have elected a Republican administration in 1952 and again in 1956. Nor does it explain the further paradox that despite the landslide victory of President Eisenhower in 1956, the Democrats won control of both houses of Congress in an unprecedented defiance of a traditional congressional majority for the party of the presidential victor. Although the winning presidential candidate usually runs somewhat ahead of his party's candidates,

Eisenhower outran his party's candidates for the House of Representatives by 9 per cent.

How party coffers are filled

The business of filling and emptying the party coffers absorbs much of every party's energies. It takes a great deal of money to run a party or campaign, even though much volunteer effort is donated. Funds are spent for office space, for mailing costs, for printing, for radio and TV time, for billboard advertising, for hall rentals, and a thousand other items, including expense money for precinct captains and local committee workers. In these days of air travel and television such expenses have become astronomical. The 1952 presidential campaigns probably cost well over $50 million, with the 1956 estimates running considerably higher.

Fundraising is indeed the hard core of any party's activity. For without funds (and the need for such funds grows larger every year) the party is soon stripped of influence. The raising and spending of money are major parts of the political process. To get the money, it is necessary to fan partisan enthusiasm in millions of hearts. But it is also necessary to ask for the money; it does not roll in unsolicited. And it is asked for in every conceivable fashion.

Friend is tapped to approach friend. Fundraising events, complete with prestige and party recognition, help to milk the party regulars. These can be affairs costing well above $100 a plate, or more modest "bean suppers," or party picnics, or even "silver" teas. Admission is charged and/or the hat is passed. And often the advance sale of tickets—which may or may not be used—goes on at high gear over many days and weeks.

Political club membership fees are also favored ways of bringing a regular flow of funds for party purposes. But at election time the need for funds skyrockets and every conceivable resource is squeezed dry. The business of building and combing prospect lists goes on ceaselessly. The names on them are bombarded with a rising tide of pleas and supplications. Often these are personally engineered—by visits and by telephone as well as through the mails. Fundraising letters signed by celebrities stuff the mailboxes of every party sympathizer in the days before election. And often after elections the same sort of fundraising has to go on to liquidate the deficit that usually faces the defeated party.

House-to-house canvassing is sometimes attempted and special appeals are dreamed up. The Democrats in 1956 engineered a "Dollar for Democrats Day." The Republicans matched this effort by a "Happy Birthday, Mr. President" fundraising drive. The sale of campaign buttons and insignia has become a big business. The parties and their candidates vie with each other in the variety, the size, and the would-be originality of their offerings.

All such efforts are supported by publicity build-ups. The skills of the advertisers and the reach of television now play an enormous part in the calculations of parties and their candidates.

The cost of campaigning has become so high and reports of undue pressure and other scandals so numerous that there has been rising clamor for public regulation. Serious citizens have become concerned lest the costs of running for public office will deter honest citizens of modest means, and state legislatures and the Congress have been pushed into regulating various aspects of party financing. Besides the Hatch Acts, and the so-called "little Hatch Acts" passed by state legislatures, corporations are prohibited from contributing to party funds in national elections, and political activities of trade unions have likewise been circumscribed. Attempts have been made to put ceilings on the amount which an individual can contribute. Such legislation, however, has had less than the desired effect. Its intent is circumvented by the establishment of a number of *ad hoc* organizations supporting the same candidate. The AFL and the CIO political action and election auxiliaries were independently incorporated in order to side-step legal disbarments from political activity; in recent years serious questions have been raised as to whether direct contributions from union treasuries of dues money from all workers are not, in fact, legal violations.

Attempts to limit candidates' expenditures also have failed to achieve their goal. National law puts a top limit of $3 million for each national committee in a presidential year. It also sets a limit of $25,000 on campaign expenses of senators; however, in these times of high costs these are unrealistic figures, and candidates often spend many times the legal amount through the device of establishing a number of special committees. Legislation is now contemplated which would put a top limit on the total amount to be spent on behalf of a given candidate by all his supporters, this limit to be set by a sliding scale which takes numbers of constituents into account.

So far no really satisfactory answer to the problem of campaign expenditures has been found. Philip L. Graham, publisher of the *Washington Post and Times-Herald,* has suggested that mass contributions from the public be solicited. He proposes a public service campaign for $5 gifts to be made to the party of the donor's choice. Such a plan, he believes, could meet the astronomical cost of campaigning without opening the parties or their standardbearers to some of the unhealthy pressures to which they are now exposed—such as the large campaign gifts routinely made by underworld sources, special-interest groups, and other favor seekers. A Gallup poll suggests that some 16 million families would be quite willing to make $5 political contributions, and in 1956 the Advertising Council announced a willingness to conduct such a nationwide nonpartisan public service campaign for party funds.

Some critics of current party financing have proposed that the government finance election campaigns, and at least one state finances some campaign literature; but government financing of campaigns is fraught with danger. Careful audit and mandatory publication of political expenditures is being increasingly required, but the enormously difficult problem of party financing will be with us for some time to come.

Why two parties?

Most Americans believe not only in parties but also in the two-party system. There are good historical reasons for this belief. The two major parties are so big that they dwarf potential opposition. Splinter parties have cropped up all through our history, but only a handful have played important roles; the Silver Party in the 1890s, the Farmer Labor Party in Minnesota, and the Progressives in 1948 all created a stir. Nearly all third parties have split off the trunk of one of the two major parties. In this sense all parties have grown from splinters, even the present Republican and Democratic parties. Splinter parties sometimes start out brilliantly but usually they soon sputter out, and this history of failure now helps to stack the cards against new third-party bids. However, third-party threats continue to be made. Such rumors, for example, gathered separately around Senator McCarthy and the Dixie-crat bloc during 1956. And President Eisenhower, unhappy with the lack of support given many of his proposals by the Republican Congress in 1952, is reported to have considered the possibility of forming a third party. "Hot" issues become meat for third-party irregulars; these often center around some special panacea, such as the Townsend pie-in-the-sky pension plan of the 1930s.

Most Americans think that it is a good thing that third parties cannot easily take root. They believe that our national two-party system serves the needs of democratic government better than either a multi-party or single-party system. Europe's experience has strengthened this view. The Nazis and the Communists have demonstrated that dire results can stem from single-party power. On the other hand, the experience of nations like France does not tempt the United States to develop a large number of parties. France has well over a dozen parties, and none can claim a majority. An unending succession of stalemates and unstable coalition governments has been the result; and there have been more than a score of governments formed since the war. No party leader can long hold so unruly a coalition together, and government headaches become chronic when neither official nor party can speak for a controlling segment of opinion.

In our two-party system there is always a chance to throw the rascals out peacefully, and it takes no bloody revolution or *coup d'état* to change the set of our government. A shift in party control will do it, as it did in the thirties and again in 1952. The pendulum swing that brings the opposition party to the top is the traditional American way of meeting new challenges and of righting old wrongs, and it keeps the opposition party on its toes. As the balance shifts, the moving consensus is constantly restructured without violent change or wholesale repudiation. Thus mercifully many differences between the parties are in details only. Both parties are bedded in a solid core of belief in the mechanism of majority vote, respect for rights of minorities, and devotion to a two-party system.

WHEN POLITICS BY-PASS THE PARTIES

The fact that the two parties so color our national life should not lead to the conclusion that there is no role for citizen action outside the parties. Any kind of citizen action that affects the operation of any part of the government process is *ipso facto* political. There is lots of such action outside the parties and some of it causes them a good deal of trouble. Americans are skillful at avoiding being cubbyholed in politics as elsewhere. They may often be "other-directed," but they are also capable of maverick tendencies.

Nonpartisan politics

In some circles nonpartisanship is the approved form of political behavior. In fact independents are sometimes so enamored of their individuality that they overlook the fact that the very existence of a public-serving party system depends on powerful antagonists. This in turn implies responsible partisanship. Of course, there is always a role for nonpartisan protest against misused party hegemony, but it takes wisdom and political know-how to assess the value of such a protest. While there are undoubtedly situations in which nothing less than a powerful dissent can deter a power-driven clique, nonpartisanship has its hazards as well as its opportunities. The citizen-politician needs to be able to size up and, if necessary, march confidently through all sorts of political smoke screens—including those raised by independents.

The fact that both parties are wedded to the two-party system means that certain issues—at least temporarily—are above the heat of partisan battle. The issues that are beyond partisanship can range from such purely local matters as garbage collection to great issues of international policy upon which the nation's life depends. Neither set of issues is by its nature removed from partisan strife, and both are often its focus. But at any one time many, indeed perhaps most, civic issues are free from burning controversy. Many of the duties of city and country governments—activities we call public housekeeping—are of this variety. As long as they are reasonably well carried out, they do not become foci for party quarrels. But if any operation is conspicuously mishandled the opposition will be happy to make a party matter of it. In such cases an ideological line may be absent. The focus will be the efficiency of the administration, or the greed and misbehavior of an individual, clique, or organization.

There are other issues which are beyond partisanship, either because the parties are willing to compromise, or simply because both are involved with more impelling matters. In fact, in times of extreme crisis, notably in wartime, the parties close ranks on most major issues. While issues temporarily above partisanship can quickly become the center of public attention, and it is seldom safe for any party to become complacent, yet it would be impossible for government to operate if its routine business were always subject to a storm of public discussion and partisan pressures.

The device of the *nonpartisan* election has been invented to remove local issues and offices from the hurly-burly of national party politics. In a number of cities aldermen, councilmen, mayors, or other major city officials are selected at these nonpartisan elections. In such cases the party designation is absent from the ballot. Sometimes the nonpartisan character of such elections is more apparent than real, since most candidates have recognized partisan connections. In Chicago, for example, in 1957 there were thirty-eight "nonpartisan" Democratic aldermen, eleven "nonpartisan" Republicans, and only one truly nonpartisan independent. In over a thousand municipalities nonpartisan city manager government is in operation.

In many communities the national party labels have in fact become meaningless in local elections. In Detroit, for example, Michigan law specifically provides by charter (adopted in 1918) that "no ballot used at any city election shall have printed thereon any party or political designation or mark, and there shall not be appended to the name of any candidate any such party or political designation or mark or anything showing how he is nominated or indicating his views or opinions." In Kansas City a nonpartisan group has repeatedly elected a majority of the City Council against the opposition of the remnants of Pendergast's Democratic machine. In Cincinnati a nonpartisan group was successful against a Republican machine. Certain other local officials, such as those of special districts, are also frequently elected on non-partisan ballots. In all such local elections nonpartisanship does not really imply lack of partisanship; rather it connotes lack of *national* party partisanship.

Nonpartisanism is also implemented in some areas by such practices as cross-filing, which allow candidates to file in both party columns on the ballot. Thus, Chief Justice Earl Warren was elected governor of California on both the Republican and the Democratic tickets. Occasionally nonpartisanship takes on a genuine fusion character. A combination of dissident Republicans and Democrats elected La Guardia mayor of New York in 1933, breaking the strongly entrenched hold of Democratic Tammany Hall. A similar movement in Philadelphia elected Mayor Joseph Clark. This kind of fusion has made itself felt as an answer to machine rule in a number of cities. Its failure in Chicago left that city with the dubious distinction of being the last great metropolitan stronghold of the old-style party machine. Paddy Bauler, a picturesque alderman of the old school, made the most quoted comment on the 1955 fusion effort: "Chicago ain't ready for reform yet."

"Pressure groups" in politics

Parties are not the only purveyors and organizers of political power. Other groups, particularly economic interest groups, carry much weight in the political picture. The larger the group and the better organized it is, the heavier its political weight. Labor, business, and agriculture feed a tremendous number of opinion-forming groups. The newly merged AFL-CIO has nearly 16 million members. The American Farm Bureau Federation, the National Grange, and the Farmer's Union and other farm organizations have memberships that total many millions. Trade associations, such as chambers of commerce and the associations of manufacturers, also have huge memberships. All of these groups exercise political power.

Political weight is swung by noneconomic groups as well. Racial and religious groups are important opinion-forming clusters. Service groups, civic organizations, veterans' groups, and recently, organizations of "senior citizens" exert significant political pressures. Each such group in its own way organizes one facet of the opinion-forming process and often flexes powerful political muscles, even though it may not exist for purely political purposes.

At the political level there have been, besides today's two major parties, an endless succession of lesser parties such as the Whigs, the Tories, the Abolitionists, the Prohibitionists, the Laborites, the Socialists, the Progressives, and, until recently outlawed, the Communists. There are also the independents, the near-independents, and the pseudo-independents. The CIO and the AFL both spawned political offshoots: the CIO Political Action Committee and Labor's League for Political Education, now combined into one group. Taxpayers' associations dot the political landscape hopefully trying to keep taxes under tight rein. And better-government associations ebb and flow across the national scene. An impressive number of limited special-interest groups maintain professional lobbyists on Capitol Hill in Washington, and hang in clusters outside state legislative chambers. There are also all sorts of *ad hoc* groups that rise phoenix-like in the wake of some torrid issue. Most of these soon wither away, but while they live they can breathe political fire. Political organizations may operate nationally or locally, or both. The Americans for Democratic Action have local affiliates in many areas. A determinedly nonpartisan group, the League of Women Voters, has a national office, forty state leagues, and more than 950 local branches.

All such groups use and are used by democratic government. They can make their weight felt as no individual can. When they complement each other and pull together their power can be great. Not infrequently, however, they collide

noisily, defeating each other and sometimes themselves. Organizational patterns continually change, and there are always
vast areas of nonorganization.

All of these groups—private, professional, and public—meet
in the political arena; their members are, after all, citizens of
the body politic. The process of developing consensi out of
this welter of diversity is the test of popular government.
Groups must be loosely harnessed through their own consent
to common political objectives, and the strands of this political
web can become tangled. One person may belong to many
groups and not all of these will see eye-to-eye on specific
political issues. And a private individual may sometimes differ
with the stand taken by a group without wishing to withdraw
from the group. This right to differ is shielded by our tradition of freedom of conscience, assembly, and speech. Yet the
fact is that somehow some degree of public consensus develops
on numberless issues. The overlapping and contradictory ideas
of all sorts of groups are tossed into the melting pot of political
democracy and a common denominator must be found before
popular government can move purposefully in any direction.

It is not surprising that there is widespread cynicism concerning the possibility of working out practicable, continuing
compromises, for such cynicism finds rich soil in the cross pull
of special interests. Yet we would be lost without specialized
groups in this complex century; for in their matrix a single
individual can feel his hand upheld, his voice strengthened,
his feeble force flowing into a swelling tide. The political
whole is often greater than the sum of its parts. Even at his
most influential, one person is just one person. Legally, at
least, he has just one vote, but his weight becomes significant
if he can coax other people to his side of the scale. This sometimes must be done by person-to-person missionary work, but
it goes forward much more rapidly if whole groups can be
converted.

All groups that flex political muscles are *per se* pressure groups. This term carries an aura of odium, but not all pressure groups are clay-footed. Whether a given group exercises good or bad pressures is a question of fact and value judgment. Group objectives and their methods must be weighed, for democracy does not accept the view that the end justifies the means. It is at this point that our political philosophy departs most sharply from that of the Communists. We deeply believe that men must be, in the Kantian idiom, "ends in themselves, not means to ends." Since both ends and means come into play in all political operations, they become important parts of the inside story of every group.

Pressure groups and their lobbyists have been a favorite whipping boy for the press and for civic groups. There has been widespread clamor that they should be severely regulated, or even abolished. The furor over actions of lobbyists for the 1956 version of the natural gas bill focused attention on lobbying problems, and brought demands for reform. There is no denying that some groups have powerfully, and sometimes illegally, influenced legislators and administrators. But many so-called pressure groups have actually worked in the public interest by upholding dedicated public officials.

Many organizations such as the League of Women Voters, the Civic Federation (a taxpayers group), the Citizens Schools Committee, the City Club, and the Citizens of Greater Chicago were of immeasurable aid in the effort to reform Chicago's politics. And special interest groups, such as labor unions, businessmen's associations, or professional groups, can always be useful on governmental issues *if* their efforts are properly evaluated. The chains of many outmoded state constitutions have been loosened by coalitions of such groups, and other electoral reforms have been achieved in the same fashion. Most legislators cannot have enough staff assistance to do thorough research on all the matters which come before them, and the so-called pressure groups often gather pertinent material. If the legislator can weigh their merits, he may have access to important data. In fact, one can make a good case for more pressure groups, since they mean that large numbers of people are taking real interest in government problems and are making their views known.

Frequently the ability to carry a private group with one is the best way of exercising political leverage. Thus the citizen-politician should be able to find his way around among the groups that figure in the political picture. He should understand not only their respective roles in public affairs but also their internal structure and power patterns. He should exercise sharp judgment as to where it is legitimate in his own interest to use these groups, or to let them use him. Groups are political molecules, and the citizen must understand their structures in order to make maximum use of the forces contained in them. Such groups train their members in the ways of democratic living and they provide a kind of apprenticeship for larger political action. All of the processes of government go on in microcosm in every group: Officers are elected; divergent views battle for acceptance; policies are voted up or down. Familiar rules of the game, not essentially different from those of politics, hold these encounters within loose bounds. In theory, at least, officers are responsible to voters (members), and the majority rules. While it is true that such rules are often honored chiefly in the breach, they live on to fight another day. The citizen can find valuable experiences in the processes of government by being an active part of a pressure group.

Locating the foci of political power

Within each group in or out of government a kind of power structure emerges. The reins are held by key personalities, usually in key positions. Rank-and-file members need to understand clearly where the real authority rests. They should know to whom to turn to get things done—and the target is always human. The process of exerting pressure goes on in and out of politics. Citizens must be able to find the points at which their influence can be exerted. Their key targets will be the decision makers who have the power to put resources behind a chosen course of action.

Policy makers on the ballot are one of the obvious foci for their attention, but channels to appointive officials should not be overlooked. They can have enormous power; indeed administrative power has grown with the scale of government operations and with the multiplication of political perplexities. Some administrative officers (like the President of the United States, the governors of states, and the mayors of cities) are elected, but the great majority of administrators are appointed. In the natural course of administrative events they wield great influence and have great responsibilities. All of the daily working decisions are theirs, for they keep the government machinery running. Such workaday tasks add up to a tremendous total of activity at every level of government. Important policy decisions are made in every corner of government and flow through the chain of command. Policy at one level becomes an administrative directive to the next. On a narrowing scale, decision making is carried on at each level on the organization chart and the process keeps right on going down to the last clerk. Everyone who makes the decisions which concern you, the citizen, is a logical target for your persuasiveness.

It is often necessary to look behind the scenes to find the really powerful figure; this, indeed, is the traditional position occupied by the great political bosses. Some of the most powerful of them have never held public office; they find their satisfactions—and sometimes substantial material rewards—by holding tight strings on men they have put into positions of power.

The process of "pressuring" is always personal as well as organizational. The key person may be the most reasonable of men, willing and anxious to go along with responsible citizen demands. He may be a born leader who knows how to play by ear—how to keep no more than one short step ahead of his constituents. But he may also be obstinate, ruthless, and self-seeking, not to be deflected from a stubborn course unless his personal armor is pierced. In any event it is never safe to ignore the personal equation. In your efforts to influence the policy makers, you need answers to these key questions: What kind of men are they? What do they really want? To whom do they listen? How do I reach them? The answers will provide a key to their attitudes toward group responsibility and their probable reaction to your persuasions.

Pressure points, of course, are partially defined by structure, but the impact of personality cannot be confined to penciled boxes on organization charts and political influence is not susceptible to precise measurement or sure control. Sometimes it boils down to the development of rapport. The ability to operate in this somewhat nebulous and intuitive area is a priceless political skill. The men who make political legend are the ones who can win friends and influence people. The amateur politician—and the plain citizen seeking to do his political bit—should never underestimate the power of personal influence. Sometimes the amateur will get a better reception than the professional whose motives may be suspected.

Even a political maverick, whose activities are often an irritation to the regular politicians, can manage to deliver for his constituents. The regulars in Chicago often used to ask: "How come Merriam is getting so many improvements for his ward when we aren't getting them?" The answer was that he had learned to put a finger on the right power source. Sometimes this meant getting around a department chief; sometimes it meant the careful build-up of a good case. If there was a magic formula, it consisted in finding a sensitized pressure point and exerting the right kind of persuasion. The moral of this story is: "Go where the real power is and line it up on your side."

The human equation in politics—as elsewhere—is crucial. *You* may say, "That's obvious," but *we* could recite instance after instance where well-intentioned citizens did not remember this basic fact of political life. Citizens would also do well to remember that public officials—and party leaders—are human beings with their own rights and feelings. Officials are rightly subject to criticism if they are arbitrary, short, rude, or dishonest. But citizens, if they want to be persuasive, should also eschew such behavior. Nor will they endear themselves by treating public officials as drones, crooks, or loafers, or by overlooking the fact that most public servants are skilled, dedicated, and underpaid, craving only a little recognition for the job they are doing.

Citizens are frequently baffled and distressed because they do not seem to be able to make a dent on official action. They watch with bewilderment, disappointment, and irritation the way in which lobbyists and other old hands confidently accomplish their objectives. The inexperienced citizen-politician is likely to jump to the conclusion that "there is something phony going on." But the controlling fact may be that professional suggestions are accepted because past associations and carefully built rapport have smoothed the path. If you get the brush-off on a maiden voyage into the political stream, remember the personal equation!

TOWARD A MORE RESPONSIBLE TWO-PARTY SYSTEM

Debate over the merits of the two-party system never ends. Obvious weaknesses, particularly in the feeblest links, lend weight to the arguments of those who are looking for a major realignment, or even minor reforms. In particular situations, the issues are often heated and major storms can center around national party responsibility at the local level; it happened in Chicago in 1955.

It is often argued that the recruiting and organization of national party workers in the localities depends on a strong parallel local organization. Where great numbers of jobs in local government are available to the party faithful, the national party has indeed a big stake in local party organization. If, however, local governments are run by civil servants under a merit system, without political patronage, then the impact of the national parties at the local level is lessened. However, the existence of strong national party groups in communities with no local patronage is strong evidence that patronage is not the only issue.

The issue of party responsibility at all levels deserves serious attention. There has been perhaps too great a tendency to reduce such responsibility. Whatever their virtues, many so-called reforms—such as cross-filing and the open primary (see Chapter Four)—actually reduce national party responsibility. Tepid turnouts at elections and the difficulty of getting good people to run for party office are dangerous symptoms of weakness in the functioning of the two-party system. In recent years students of government have been concerned lest the national two-party system suffer serious erosion. They are suggesting that it be strengthened and that its machinery be made more adaptable. A committee of the American Political Science Association has suggested the following steps to strengthen the parties:

1. Biennial party conventions
2. Interim party councils (with powers considerably greater than those of present national committees)
3. Development of intraparty organization, including regional arrangements
4. Coordination of platforms at various levels of government, with more binding platform commitments
5. Improvement of party organization in Congress
6. Wider political participation by the citizenry
7. Improved nominating procedures
8. Improved electoral processes
9. Stepped up party research
10. More responsible party leadership.[2]

[2] "Toward a More Responsible Party System," Supplement to *American Political Science Review* (September 1950), p. 1.

Steps have already been taken to implement some of these objectives. Party publications such as the *Democratic Digest* and the Republicans' new "newspaper" are expounding the "party lines." The national committees have stepped up their work in the years between elections. Regional conferences of party officials and officeholders are held more frequently. More intensive effort is being made to recruit citizen-politicians into party activities. All of these are deliberate efforts to build greater responsibility into the two-party system.

Party loyalty however can be overdone, particularly if it results in dangerous fissures in the body politic. It has been argued that the very looseness of our national party organizations is a valuable democratic asset. There are few Americans who would relish the thought of two parties sharply divided on class, religious, or other grounds. But there is also a danger that the parties will move the other way, becoming too diffuse to serve as strong rallying points. The political independent has often played a useful role in helping force the parties to take firm positions. He acts as a kind of gadfly; but neither he nor his organization can take over the full reach of the functions of the major parties.

One thing is clear: To do their job today parties need the participation of increasing numbers of citizen-politicians. To get the work of politics done, parties are and must be major rallying points. Yet they must not be allowed to polarize civic differences to the extent that they become permanently unreconcilable. Each of us has a vital job to do in helping our two-party system maintain the momentum which keeps pushing the civic consensus ahead of it. Parties are the best mechanism we have been able to invent to magnify individual voices and views. One vote—channeled and multiplied in party action—becomes more than an insignificant statistic. It is the task of the citizen-politician to see that his party speaks well and truly for him.

CHAPTER FOUR

The Citizen and Political Decisions—
Leaders and Issues

Since the exercise of governmental power is a prime political target any party will naturally give close attention to the selection (and, hopefully, the control) of public officials. The prerogatives of government are exercised by key individuals, and the parties want to be sure that these posts are occupied by *their* men, who see the issues as they do. They also want to control as many of the minor posts as possible, if only to reward the party faithful. It is no wonder then that jobs gleam luminously before the eager gaze of every party man and the *nomination, election, appointment,* and *control* of public officials is a first concern of the parties.

PARTIES AND THE SELECTION OF LEADERS

Over the years the parties have developed many ways of trying to control the selection process. Some of these have worked in the public interest, but occasionally they have not. Citizens need to be alert to perennial efforts of inside cliques to try to control the selection process in their own interests. Public law repeatedly has had to be marshaled to safeguard the democratic selection of public officials; many facets of the nomination process and even party procedures are now closely regulated. Such regulation centers around three preferred methods of nomination:

1. By party convention
2. By direct primary election
3. By petition

It is in the public interest to see that all three methods permit real popular control, for a broad popular base under party or other nominations is essential to democratic functioning.

Nomination by convention

Candidates for the presidency are nominated by conventions of the parties, and many states such as New York also select such key nominees as governor in party convention. The delegates to the national conventions are selected in a variety of ways. Some are directly elected by party voters in the primaries and are authorized to vote as they choose. Others, also elected, are committed to vote for a specified candidate. Still others are guided but not controlled by the outcome of a presidential preferential primary. Finally, some delegates are appointed by party officials, under local regulations. Every state and territory is represented, but their weight in the balloting depends on local party turnout in previous elections. The presidential nominating conventions are attended by from three to five thousand delegates and alternates.

These conventions occupy the center of public attention for many weeks. The groundwork for their activities—and their hullabaloo—takes months of work, thousands of people, and millions of dollars. They are colorful, extravagant, even raucous exhibitions. Speeches sometimes reach oratorical heights and occasionally slide to the depths of demagoguery. There is wearisome repetition: "Mr. Chairman, the great and fair state of——deems it a privilege to put into nomination the name of its favorite son, a man whose record has brought honor and fame to this illustrious commonwealth . . ." and so on and on into the smoke-filled, hot summer nights. The weaving dance of the banner-waving, shouting paraders, the blare of the loudspeakers, clusters of gesticulating, pleading, perspiring men forming and reforming on the floor—all this has been brought into millions of living rooms through television. For days the public has a front-row seat, thanks to the inexhaustible prying of the newsmen and their microphones and cameras. As a nation we have learned much; for this is a phenomenon which until recently was viewed only by the delegates and convention visitors. We have come to understand the political uses—and abuses—of parliamentary procedures. We have watched political statures and political fortunes grow and shrivel. Emotions are sometimes laid uncomfortably bare. At the climax we see and hear the acceptance speeches of the presidential and vice-presidential candidates, the standard bearers for their parties.

These national conventions duplicate on a larger stage similar procedures all over the nation. Party conventions are held at county, state, and district levels at the discretion of the parties—or occasionally as provided by law. In every case the delegates select standard bearers, set policies, and conduct the party business. Procedures at all conventions are woven through with party traditions and rules, and increasingly with legislative prohibitions and regulations. An interesting study of power structures and decision-making at the 1952 national conventions was made under the auspices of the American Political Science Association.[1]

Primaries: open and closed

With increasing frequency party nominees, delegates to party conventions, and party officials are being selected in

[1] P. J. David, M. Moos, and R. M. Goldman, *Presidential Nominating Politics in 1952* (Baltimore: Johns Hopkins Press, 1954).

public elections. Such publicly supervised party elections—primaries—are now widespread; only nine states are without them.

Primaries were introduced to eliminate the abuses that grew up in the convention system in the late 1800s and early 1900s. In those free-swinging days the wishes of ordinary party members were often blatantly ignored, and party bosses and their machines took over the conventions. The public finally became outraged and undertook to try to enforce open, honest, and democratic party nominating procedures. One state after another passed laws which provided that nominees for key posts should be selected through publicly supervised party primary elections.

Primaries are of two kinds—open and closed. In the *open primary* the names of candidates of both parties appear on the same ballot, and the voter makes a choice without revealing his party affiliation. In a *closed primary* the voter receives only the ballot of his own party and must therefore publicly declare his party preference.

Closed primary laws attempt to strengthen party organization and responsibility by making the nominating procedure more directly responsive to the wishes of the whole party. But even in states with closed primaries, ingenious voters have found ways to get around this intent. Voters and organizations soon learned to hop from primary to primary in successive elections. If, for example, there was little or no contest in the Republican primary and a bitter one in the Democratic primary, the Republican organization might well counsel its members to vote in the Democratic primary to insure the selection of the candidate who would be easiest for the Republicans to beat. To prevent this sort of tactical jumping about, primary legislation in some states has been still further tightened. In a number of states a citizen can vote in the primary of the opposing party only if a minimum number of months have passed since his last primary vote. Thus, in order to change parties, he must usually abstain from voting in some intervening primary election.

Such voting limitations have no carry-over into the actual election, though there has often been public confusion on this point. Such confusion was deliberately fostered in the 1955 mayoral election in Chicago. The fact is that any voter can vote a straight party ticket or split his votes among the parties, and none be the wiser; at least that is the theory, although the practice is sometimes undercut by unscrupulous pressures.

The right to a place on the ballot: nomination by petition

Tightened primary laws have taken nominating procedures a substantial way down the road to popular control by safeguarding the interests of party members. Still other legal safeguards have been set up to protect the rights of candidates to run for office and the rights of citizens to vote for nonorganization candidates.

Candidates may win a place on most ballots by filing petitions with the election authorities. These petitions must carry the signatures of a prescribed number of voters. The method, procedure, and the timing of filing of such petitions is spelled out in great detail. Party say-so is no longer enough to insure a place on most ballots; a modicum of public support must also be demonstrated. The number of required signatures is usually a specified percentage of the registered voters of an area, but it may be determined by the number of votes cast in the last equivalent election. The requirements for nomination of party officials by petition may vary widely within the same state. Thus in one state:

Office	*Required Signatures*
Delegate to national nominating convention	½ of 1% of electors in congressional district
State central committeemen	100 electors in congressional district

Precinct committeemen	10 electors in district
Township committeemen	5–8% of electors
Ward committeemen	10–17% of electors

Independent voters may have to meet still other, and stiffer, requirements as witness the regulations in another jurisdiction:

Office	Required Signatures for Independent Voters
State office	25,000 votes (at least 200 for each of 50 counties)
City officials	5–8% of votes cast in district at last general election (25 minimum)
Alderman	2% of votes cast in district (25 minimum)

It is far easier for the regular party candidates to get their petitions filled than for independents; for the parties are geared to signature-collecting. When the word goes out that "Janowitz is in," signatures for his petitions are quickly gathered by the faithful toilers of the party. The independent candidate almost inevitably has to work up his own organization in order to get his petitions filled. Persistent mavericks can and do get on the ballot, whether the party organization likes it or not, but it is an uphill task. Extra-party nominations by petition are most frequent in those areas where there are nonpartisan elections (mostly in cities) or in elections where minor party candidates or independents seek to get around a party's slatemaking.

Independent candidates and the write-in vote

Our system of popular elections provides—theoretically at least—that any legally qualified person shall be allowed to run for any office. As might be imagined, party cliques sometimes try to make this difficult. Election laws reflect the outcome of the pulling and hauling between such special interests and those of the general public. And results vary widely. In some places third parties are permitted to have their own party primary or convention if the party or its candidates received a specified percentage of the total vote in a preceding election. Minor-party candidates—or independent candidates—cannot often meet these specifications, and in order to have their names appear on the ballot they must file petitions usually carrying large numbers of signatures. In the Chicago mayoralty election, the Merriam backers had to give serious consideration to such technical matters. If their candidate ran in a primary of one of the major parties, he needed only a few thousand signatures. But if he by-passed the primaries and ran in the election as an independent candidate, he had to have over eighty thousand signatures. This requirement was an important consideration in his decision *not* to run as an independent.

The form and detail of petitions are frequently rigidly regulated. Thus in many jurisdictions first names must usually be spelled out in full; "Avenue" may not be abbreviated; "East" must be used instead of "E."; the name of the county must be included, and so forth. There are always time limits attached to the filing of nominating petitions, if for no other reason than to allow time to print and distribute the ballots. In some places petitions must be filed as much as eighty-five days before the election. Sometimes the time limits are somewhat elastic, and deadlines are extended if a party is willing to pay the price of reprinting the ballots.

Any breach of regulations, however minor—even an accidental mistake—can disqualify a signature. This has resulted in some unexpected developments. Sometimes a sardonic game develops and each party's workers try to see how many of the opposition's signatures they can throw out on technicalities.

In most jurisdictions, regardless of other nominating procedures it is possible for a citizen to nominate his own candidate by writing in that candidate's name on the ballot on election day. This is doing it the hard way, but write-in campaigns are sometimes the only way out. Charles E. Merriam, who had served three terms as alderman in Chicago and made one try for mayor, was ruled off the ballot when he ran for reelection as alderman in 1917. His supporters then staged a write-in campaign but it fell short of victory by a handful of votes.

A successful write-in candidacy did occur, however, in Chicago's aldermanic campaign of 1951. The incumbent objected to his opponent's petitions on the grounds that they contained *too many* signatures (the law, since changed, had set a maximum as well as a minimum number of names). In any event, the election board ruled that the objection was valid, and the challenger—David Muir—was denied a place on the ballot. Muir's supporters rose in arms, with wide backing from the press and civic groups. The courts were appealed to, but they ruled that they could not interfere with an administrative decision. The election board had closed four out of every five polling places in the affected ward "to save money," they said, "because there was only one name on the ballot." This was the last straw; on election day hundreds of persons walked extra blocks to the new polling places, stood in slowly moving lines, and carefully and precisely wrote "David Muir" on the ballots.

In 1954 former Governor J. Strom Thurmond, States Rights candidate for President in 1948, pulled off a minor miracle by being elected to the Senate of the United States by a write-in vote.

But whether a write-in vote wins or not, it makes its weight felt and it can shake the complacency of entrenched cliques. Write-ins appear in almost every election, if only as the work of cranks or diehards. Comic-book characters persistently make their way onto ballots; and many a lost hope has made his final brief appearance as a write-in candidate.

Write-in campaigns always run into difficulties. It is hard to shake loose the habits of those who vote the party circle as regularly as night follows day, and it is just as hard to persuade the nonvoter to go to the polls. Moreover there are high technical hurdles in the way of a write-in campaign. Each voter must be convinced that it is worth the effort, and he must be trained to engineer his vote so that it will be tallied. Write-in votes are likely to be thrown out, if only to make for easier tallying. Judges and clerks of election are appointed by the major parties and it is hardly surprising if their vigilance on behalf of write-in candidates is less than enthusiastic. They may let their preferences have a free hand, or they may simply follow the line of least resistance and overlook write-in votes. Anyone who has served on an election board in the tiring hours of a paper ballot tally knows how much simpler it is to record straight votes. The write-in candidate should always be protected by an aggressive corps of watchers.

Behind the scenes

It is worth repeating that the regulation of nominating procedures is designed to keep the process flexible enough to allow legitimate nonorganization groups and private persons to present their candidates to the public. But all the laws and regulations in the world cannot wholly protect the selection process from the determined manipulation of powerful groups. The final defense is citizen alertness. The citizen-politician must be able to understand such pressures in order—where necessary—to help undercut them. Subterranean pressures are nowhere more active than in the nomination process. Power plays are always at work; the selection process goes on long before the primaries, and often far behind the scenes.

Even legal safeguards can not always deter a strong group of insiders from finding ways to insure that their man gets on the ballot. Human beings in quest of power can twist and turn themselves through almost any network of legal restrictions, exercising the greatest ingenuity in widening loopholes. And in extreme cases corrupt political machines have been tempted to use nonlegal ways to accomplish their ends, including persuasion by threat. Power being such heady stuff, there is always a danger that *any* party organization may become ingrown and oligarchic unless the run-of-the-mill members exercise vigilance and forceful resistance. One of the danger signs of incipient machine rule is a nominating procedure that is clearly under the control of a self-perpetuating clique.

Despite all safeguards, the dominant power group in the party structure (which may or may not be a political machine) usually controls the selection of party nominees. There is often little contest; party leaders, or an inside clique, decide who will be endorsed as the regular candidate. This process is known as slatemaking. Party slatemakers, legitimate and illegitimate, operate at every level of government. They naturally believe in their own ability to select the most suitable candidates for public office, and they tend to take a dim view of the preferences of uninformed outsiders. Slatemakers may be leaders who are powers in their own right, or they may be chosen representatives of factional or organizational subunits. They may be self-appointed, ex officio, or elected. Their activities may go on in the full glare of daylight or in the dim reaches of the smoke-filled rooms. But even when the final choice shapes up as a broad party decision (in a convention or a public primary), it is often true that some committee or group has composed the slate behind the scenes. So important is slatemaking that the inner circle will, whenever possible, reserve this task to itself.

Generally a central party committee makes the final choice. Such committees function at the county, city, state, and national levels. These are usually delegate bodies, representing on some predetermined basis precincts, wards, counties, congressional districts, or states. And the voice of each delegate generally is proportionate to his vote-delivering record. To keep the slatemaking selection process open and aboveboard, public hearings are sometimes prescribed. These are intended to be genuine screenings but without vigilance they become simply window dressing for previously consummated back-stage deals. This sort of window-dressing was brought into play in Chicago in 1955.

The citizen-politician must keep a weather eye and ear out for such manipulation. This takes real sleuthing, but the opposing party is only too glad to help, and the press is a stalwart ally in ferreting out political rings within rings. A word of caution to the novice: it is unsafe and politically naïve to rely unquestioningly on the *forms* of democratic selection.

The problem of keeping inner cliques from exercising un-healthy control weaves its way through conventions as well as primaries. "King-makers" are a familiar factor at all conven-tions and smooth surfaces can overlay wells of connivance, even venality. But rigging a convention is always a major undertaking and a political hazard. The best-laid calculations can and do go awry; a promised bloc of votes is weaned away at the last moment; misunderstandings arise and fissures sud-denly appear in a supposedly solid front; and occasionally the top blows right off.

Nominations from the floor are a device which is sometimes successfully used to break the hold of the insiders, but a floor revolt always takes careful planning and promotion. Nomina-tors and seconders must be planted, parliamentary strategy carefully planned, and caucuses matched by counter-caucuses. Rumors grow and drift, and one of the knottiest problems is to keep official communication lines clear and untapped. Operations on the floor always involve masterly strategy and coordination, and successful revolt has to be at least as artfully and persistently engineered as the operations of the opposi-tion. Personal loyalties must be developed and cultivated. Strength must be assessed accurately, allies aligned, and bargains made. All of this takes skill and effort, but the reward is sometimes the upset of entrenched power.

Periodically it has been urged that the convention system be eliminated in favor of primary elections. It is true that conventions are less direct than primaries as a method of selecting party nominees, but unfortunately the record of citizen participation in direct primaries has not been distinguished. All too often they too have tended to be rubber stamps of endorsed candidates, elected by the regulars who are often the only ones to turn out on primary day. It is interesting to note in this connection that although Mayor Kennelly was the overwhelming favorite in the Democratic primary in 1955 (as indicated by the Merriam poll and several others), when the vote was counted the organization candidate—Daley—won rather easily. The answer to this riddle lies largely in the small turnout of primary voters. This example could be multiplied many times. But rebels and independents have won both in party primaries and in conventions.

There have been wide shifts in the importance of the different methods of nominating our public and party officials, and it is a heartening commentary on the vitality of the democratic process that many of the changes move in the direction of broader popular control. The course, however, is far from smooth. And it always needs the firm guiding hand of the citizen-politician.

The party caucus

Citizens are coming increasingly to recognize their stake in the nominating process and they are insisting that party practices take into account broad member and public interest. Since the closed-door session is preferred by those who would control the party, efforts are being made to keep those doors open. A lengthening list of laws and regulations attempt to insure the ventilation of the selection processes. Some of these regulations even penetrate the workings of the party *caucuses* —the planned meetings of party leaders.

A caucus, ostensibly, is more democratic than secret sessions of the self-selected. At least it is an openly scheduled meeting of party officials or other representative party groups. The caucus is an intraorganizational mechanism and appears at every level of the party, at every level of government, and notably in legislative halls. Just how accurately it represents the whole membership depends most of all on the basis of selection of its members.

Caucuses provide an orderly way of ironing out differences and of marshaling support for party action, but they can also be used as a gag on a maverick opposition. It is always a question of fact whether a given caucus actually represents its members. Its ground rules are all-important; sometimes a self-imposed *unit rule* binds all participants to support the decision of the majority. Some state delegations to the national party conventions operate under such a rule. Rules can be changed, of course, with greater or less difficulty, and like many another political invention, the caucus is as useful a tool as its members permit it to be. The citizen-politician needs to be clear on who is caucusing, what the authority of the caucus is, as well as what issues are at stake. He also needs to be ready to fight for procedures that permit a truly democratic caucus.

There is no single nominating method which guarantees democratic results. Although the party primary can be more democratic than a convention, it may also be dominated by the same entrenched groups. Many people fail to realize the importance of party primaries in our democratic machinery. They ignore them or refuse to vote on the grounds that they do not want to declare their party affiliation. And they fail most of all to realize that it is necessary to participate in both primaries and conventions if you want to influence the nominating process. Since most nominations are party nominations, the so-called independent voter who stands outside the party machinery disbars himself from full-scale participation in the nominating process.

The citizen-politician who wishes seriously to influence the selection of his party leaders will make the most of the following opportunities when they are appropriate:

Vote in the primary of his party—carefully following the rules so that his vote will not be thrown away.

Assist in circulating petitions for the candidate of his choice and engineer his own signature with careful regard for the legal requirements.

Learn how to use the write-in, where that becomes necessary.

Be alert to the processes by which nominees are actually being chosen; attend caucus sessions and party hearings to make known his interest and wishes—*in time.*

Talk about the importance of the nominating process.

Broaden his understanding of the requirements of public office and the capacities of the candidates in order to help fit square pegs in square holes.

PUBLIC POLICY AND POLITICAL ACTIVITIES

Political parties not only select candidates and elect public officials; they play a central role in the formulation and development of public policy. The day-to-day decisions of responsible politicians both build and interpret this policy. For policies as well as personalities, election day is decision day par excellence. When on that day the ordinary citizen registers his "yes" or "no," he is not only electing candidates, he is crystallizing policies—programs—and party differences.

Parties and the molding of public opinion

Parties are standard bearers for different systems of loyalty, but they are also educators of citizens. They pose the issues, promote the candidates, and drive home an understanding of government structures and operations. They give civic issues substance and immediacy and their campaigning provides education on government processes and problems. They take this education, along with the faces and voices of their candidates, directly to the citizens.

The old-time cracker-barrel forums, party rallies, and picnics have slipped in their political importance; new devices, new pressures, the mass media, and the propagandists' skills are augmenting their efforts, and in some cases replacing them. But not even a high-powered propaganda barrage can have its full impact without the support of personal pressures, particularly those of peer groups. Social acceptance by one's nearest associates always carries more weight than any honeyed voice or sparkling television performance. Television, of course, has been able to do things which newspapers, the direct-mail propagandist, and even the radio have not been able to do. It has been able to transmit a sense of immediacy that is peculiarly, and some say devilishly, effective. Personal qualities come across in a way no other medium can match; at the same time distance is narrowed and time condensed. Showmanship can be used to define and illustrate issues, or to confuse them. Alternatives are brought into living rooms. The new medium puts the old-style operator at a disadvantage, and political audiences are now measured in scores of millions.

But whatever the communications medium employed, every campaign gives rise to a propaganda barrage and the scale and reach of these activities are being stepped up all the time. The press agent or public relations expert is now standard equipment for all major contests. Just how influential such efforts are is still a moot question. Merriam and Gosnell put it this way:

Are elections won or lost in accordance with the skill or lack of skill of the party propagandists? This is a difficult question. . . . In the party primaries and in local campaigns it is likely that superior campaigning techniques may be decisive, but in presidential elections, where the floodlights of national publicity are focused on both of the major candidates, it may be that the direction of the tide of public opinion is more important than the skill of the party propagandists. When the tide is running strongly against the party which has held the presidency, as in the campaigns of 1920 and 1932 [the present authors would add 1952], it appears doubtful if any technical devices can stem it. Adverse economic conditions, an accumulation of latent animosities, and a general lack of confidence are obstacles which overwhelm the party manager. . . . Lazarsfeld and his associates showed that party propaganda is not likely to be read by those whose minds are already made up. Party publicity has a reinforcing influence. It is necessary to get out the party vote. . . . President Truman showed in 1948 what could be done by a whirlwind campaign. Commentators are agreed that he won many last minute votes.[2]

Electronics and the mass media, however, have not been able to do away with personal campaigning or the city precinct captain and his rural equivalent. The feedback of person-to-person contacts has no substitute. It used to be that newspapers and their editorials were potent enough to settle the fate of a political aspirant or a political issue, but this is no longer so true. The result of modern presidential and congressional—and even local—elections has often borne little relation to newspaper support.

Party efforts to spotlight public issues and sharpen party differences are important services to democratic government. They are an essential part of organizing the consent of the governed and carrying forward the moving consensus. But if private or narrow party considerations are put above public welfare, the result is confusion, delay, and even imperiled democratic processes. Party members should be aware of their overriding civic responsibilities and citizen-politicians should keep them toeing the line.

[2] Charles E. Merriam and Harold F. Gosnell, *American Party System*, 4th ed. (New York: The Macmillan Company, 1949), pp. 391–2.

Party platforms: fact and fancy

Party standard bearers personalize party issues; and they are guided ostensibly in policy matters by the *party platform*. Platforms appear at every level of government and they are often strong rallying points. They may be formally adopted in convention or informally accepted by use. In the course of campaigning, the policy statements of the candidates and campaign promises are dignified by the magic of the word "platform." But sometimes campaign promises bear little critical scrutiny, and even the official platforms may become nothing more than bouquets of euphemisms.

Every official, to some extent, speaks for his party, and even precinct and county workers can strongly influence party issues. Attitudes, emphases, and explanations put meat on the bones of platforms. The candidate himself is often the head carpenter in platform building. His arguments, his interpretations, even his silences and his omissions give depth and meaning to the platform; candidates have even been accused of rewriting platforms. Certainly, personal sculpturing goes on ceaselessly. It is a process that cannot always be tightly controlled from headquarters, although flagrant breaches of the party line may cause an organizational flurry or demands for public retractions. Even in the absence of a formal platform, Candidate Smith's, Jones's, or Roe's public-spirited acceptance of public and party responsibilities can hammer out a workmanlike structure. When this happens, true character and dignity enter the campaign, for such platform making is the mark of political statesmanship. It makes an important contribution to party solidarity and it gives substance to people's choices. Platforms can be brought into finer focus by responsible public discussion of issues.

Although much platform making is informal and personal, there are times when platforms are solemnly written down after much thoughtful and formal consideration. Every major convention has its platform committee, and other committees also help to shape particular planks. Party caucuses play significant roles in redefining issues, party position, and organizing a united front behind party policy.

The platform committee is a key organ of any convention, and the shaping of party planks is always tied into the selection of a candidate. The party standard bearer must at the least be able and willing to stand on his party's platform. If candidate and platform do not always work hand in glove, at least they are handcuffed to each other, and where one goes so must the other. Where there are sharp differences, the opposition is only too happy to spot this Achilles' heel of weakness and take up the refrain: "broken promises, bold-faced frauds, insincerity, inconsistency bordering on stupidity," and so forth.

Party platforms have significance even when they are encumbered with ambiguities or inconsistencies, for every party needs issues as well as candidates. Each tries to make its position widely appealing, so as to win the maximum number of votes; but each must be able to point to torchbearing differences, if for no better reason than to gather virtue unto itself and to relegate vice to the opposition. It takes expert tightrope walking at times to be all things to all people and still remain conspicuously Democratic or Republican.

Platforms are built by garnering many points of view, by sifting them for their vote-getting ability, by measuring them against traditional policy and fitting them together into some pattern of internal consistency. Somehow the planks have to be lashed together solidly enough to serve as a vehicle for the whole party. The history of political platforms has produced many anomalies. Many of the same items, in fact, have appeared in the platforms of both parties. A certain amount of this paired patriotic window dressing is to be expected, and both parties take credit for popular and successful policies.[3]

[3] Standard items for platforms have been described as follows: "All platforms include such standard items as the following: 1) eulogy of

Yet neither can afford to become a me-too party. Each must keep its identity. Thus there is always real disagreement. Sometimes tremendous heat is generated around minor issues. Sometimes differences are more apparent in the spirit of the platform than in its actual wording; and frequently the record speaks louder than the words. There are few more interesting undertakings than to compare party platforms, item by item and plank by plank. Some platforms are jerry-built; like houses of cards they lean together precariously. If one were cynical, it would be easy to say that platforms mean little, but this is not in fact true.

In one sense, it is fortunate that the rival platforms are so often in agreement, for that fact removes certain issues from the arena of partisan strife. As a consequence, whichever side wins, the other can accept with fair grace the majority decision, at least until the next election. In the working out of democratic government, such areas of hard-won agreement must always take precedence over differences.

Real differences between the platforms of our two great parties have emerged. Sometimes these are major and sometimes minor. Behind the windmill-tilting that is a familiar campaign phenomenon there lurks a force and a loyalty that is built partly on ideological differences. These may represent real or fancied class or economic interests. They may, unhappily, represent racial or other bias. Or they may simply stem from habit and the affectionate loyalty of tradition. But the fact is that differences do exist. Singly or in combination they may be quite enough to swing an election; and the combination of any two is powerful partisan ammunition.

To those who would dispose of party platforms as mere

the party's record; 2) denunciation of the opposition; 3) general declaration favoring democracy and Americanism; 4) references to the timely non-party issues; 5) non-committal reference to certain disputed issues; and 6) definite pledges." Charles E. Merriam and Robert E. Merriam, *The American Government; Democracy in Action* (New York: Ginn and Co., 1954), p. 76.

window dressing, we would point out the role that key planks have played in a number of important elections: for example, the 1948 Democratic battle over a civil rights plank. Again in 1956 the forging of the civil rights plank was the highlight of both conventions but especially of the Democrats. Party unity was clearly at stake in the resolution of that knotty issue.

A realistic understanding of platforms and platform-making can help the citizen-politican to make his contribution. He can appear at the platform hearings in person. He can help to bring organization pressure to a focus. He can buttonhole key people and transmit his ideas through influential channels, and he can even prepare policy statements for consideration by the program committee. If platforms are to be meaningful, forward-looking private citizens working within the parties of their choice must get under the platform-making load.

Public opinion and political polls [4]

The ultimate target of all election procedures is votes. Public opinion, registered primarily through the ballot box, is the final sanction, the ultimate force of democratic government. Its power is everywhere acknowledged and its approval everywhere courted. Every party figure from ward heeler and county worker to the top leader anxiously listens to its ground swell. When its mandate is clear, decisive, and united, no opposition can stand against it; when it is divided, uncertain, or diffuse, the best laid political plans will fall apart. Even dictators have a wholesome respect for it. They do everything possible to influence it in their favor; they buy it, manufacture it, and use every known device to bludgeon it into line. They are particularly vigilant to prevent unfavorable public reaction from undermining their position.

What precisely is this public opinion that is the master of every government? It has been cogently described as a force

[4] Adapted from Merriam and Merriam, *op. cit.*, pp. 91–95.

"that is born and dies every day, is young and old, faithful and unfaithful, consistent and inconsistent, reasonable and unreasonable; is courted, deceived, misled, yet sometimes righted again by some mysterious self-regulating capacity; is manipulated, yet able to manipulate its ablest manipulator; always in disagreement with itself, yet the shield of national unity." [5]

Those who wish to capitalize on its force or simply to understand it have long tried to measure it, but without complete success. Every election shapes up into a battle to capture sectors of public opinion, and campaign methods and procedures must be constantly reevaluated and refocused. The new media of communication have enormously complicated the tasks of engineering and of measuring political favor. But the final test is whether ideas and programs win voters, and in this area personal contact still remains a crucial political weapon.

The problem of building and maintaining channels of communication during a campaign is always a major one; and it has several dimensions. How are messages best transmitted? What issues should be stressed? How much should one make of the qualifications of the candidate? Or the weaknesses of the opposition? What emphasis should be put on party as against person? Solid fact on which to make such decisions is lacking, although public opinion sampling techniques have begun to untangle some of the strands of citizen response.

Opinion polls have grown rapidly in popularity and refinement. Such polls are the lineal descendants of the old-fashioned straw vote, but important new elements have been added through the development of more-or-less scientific methods. Progress in this field is making for greater reliability and more useful formulations, although sampling methods and the interpretation of their results remain storm centers of discussion. Accurate results depend on careful advance anal-

[5] K. Riezler, "What is Public Opinion?", *Social Research*, November 1944, p. 397.

ysis of the problems, skillful formulation of questions and questioning procedures, and careful and subtle analysis of the data. All of these facets of the polling process have been under close study by such organizations as the National Research Council, the Social Science Research Council, a number of learned societies, universities, and specialized organizations such as the National Opinion Research Center.

Political opinion polls have met with stormy times, particularly when they have tried to prophesy election results. The *Literary Digest* poll of 1936 fell so wide of its mark that it carried the magazine into bankruptcy. The profitable *Fortune* and Gallup polls both received bad jolts in the 1948 election. Their margins of error were small but sufficiently large to miscall that closely contested election.

Polls appear to be most useful in testing the adequacy of public information on alternative courses of action. They are also helpful in forecasting how people of different backgrounds view specific public issues. The Merriam organization used one of the most extensive opinion polls ever employed in a local election. Four different surveys were made: in October 1954, January 1955, March 1955, and (after the election) in late April and early May 1955. Questions were directed at candidate popularity, at the importance of particular issues, at reactions to the changing campaign situation, at reasons for not voting, and so forth. Reactions to issues that developed in the course of the campaign were most interesting. Voting irregularities and ghost voting had been widely discussed. Eighty-two per cent of the persons interviewed reported that they had heard of these issues. Seven per cent of all those interviewed did not believe the stories. Another 5 per cent reported that they were aware of the stories but were unaffected by them in any way. Nearly half of the interviewees believed the stories but still said their vote was not influenced by them. Such data indicated that the issue of voting irregularities had no great draw. The same polls also showed that a deciding factor in this election was party loyalty—in this case, to the Democratic party. They also indicated that party loyalty was most potent among Negro voters. One voter told an interviewer after the election that he had contributed money to Merriam's campaign, but could not bring himself to go to the polls because Merriam was listed as a Republican!

The results of preelection polls were used to help give direction to the campaign. The October 1954 polls had indicated that people were interested in physical problems affecting Chicago. Traffic and transportation ranked first, followed by housing and sewage, a byproduct of a rash of flooded basements. The third poll, two weeks before election, accurately forecast the election defeat. Its results were kept from the workers so that morale would not be dampened during the last hectic days of the campaign. A newspaper straw poll showing a slow trend toward Daley had already sufficiently discouraged some Merriam workers, as it no doubt had accelerated the efforts of the opposition. Thus public opinion polls contribute a new element of hazard to campaigning. President Truman, however, refused to be discouraged by the 1948 polls that showed him losing to Dewey. He simply stepped up his very personal campaign—and upset the polls.

Opinion polls will play an increasingly important part in the calculations of political parties and government officials. But fear that they will take the place of decision-making through elections and legislative action is exaggerated. Off-the-cuff answers to impersonally put questions will never replace trained judgment in guiding our vastly complicated mechanism of government. Public opinion is always the final forum; in democratic government it is expressed finally as the consent of the governed. It stands to the side, remaining something over and above any of its obvious manifestations and all of its manipulators. Its power is recognized, but its control remains illusive. Indefinable but all-powerful, it is an entity that no group or groups can completely capture. It is the voice of the moving consensus that gives democracy its ultimate power. The knowing and determined citizen-politician can help to make that voice loud, clear, and harmonious.

CHAPTER FIVE

A Citizen's Eye-View of the Ballot Box

DECISION BY VOTE

The ballot box stands in the center of the political picture. Around it swirl the eddies of political life, and on it are focused the eyes and ears of every party stalwart. It is the final arbiter of public consent, the mechanism by which majority will is brought to focus. Public issues and the operation of government machinery hang in the balance in every election; so does the education of citizens, for voters are always subjected to intensive bombardments of public issues and party panaceas. The ballot box is clearly the Mecca for the parties and it is the measuring stick of political control even for a political machine. Wins and losses, jobs, prestige, power, even social and economic progress—or its opposite—are registered in it. It is a kind of filtering device which helps to untangle the strands of popular choice, sorting out the politically possible from the politically unacceptable. As the polls close, popular leadership and popular mandates float to the top, and the victorious party takes up the reins of government. The ballot box puts personal and party fortunes into the framework of a much larger picture. Sometimes a public issue is directly voted up or down, but generally the process of public decision is more devious,

133

and issues become entangled with the political fortunes of particular candidates.

The lives of the parties are closely tied to the ballot box; so is the course of government. For the party official it is the barometer which measures the effectiveness of political activities. For the candidate it is the pathway to public office and it also spells out the mandate of the electorate. Unless one understands elections, the details of party structure and operation are meaningless. Unless one sees the voting process in the round one cannot effectively use one's personal political weight to help tip the scales of democratic government.

Thus the ballot box is the obvious place to start taking a hand in things political. Minimum civic duty surely starts here, and the citizen who is prepared to walk through the ballot box, in the best Alice-in-Wonderland tradition, will find himself in a political world as exciting—and as surprising—as any conjured up by the fertile brain of Lewis Carroll. The business of affixing X's where they will do the most good is far from simple. It takes more than a million elected officials to run our complicated system of national, state, and local governments. Often scores of names appear on a single ballot. Many issues too are decided in the voter's booth, when propositions are placed on the ballot. Bond issues, amendments to state constitutions, propositions of all sorts that require public ratification appear on ballots. Sometimes such items are printed on separate proposition ballots. Sometimes they are printed on the face of the candidates' ballot. Sometimes they appear in simple clear phrases in large print, but more often they are set forth as legal abstractions and appear in small print. In any case they play an important role in the business of self-government—and further complicate the task of decision by citizen-politicians.

Assessing the issues and candidates

How can one intelligently vote under such circumstances?

How effective can an individual citizen's preference be? Short of giving up in unhappy frustration, the easiest course for the citizen is to follow a "party line," like a puppet on a string. But there is little comfort and less effective citizenship in dancing automatically to the party's tune. Choosing a party intelligently does not mean passively accepting all its candidates and its stands on all issues. The civic-minded citizen who scorns "feather-bedding" will find real satisfaction in deepened understanding of the political process, in keener insight into political personages, and in rewarding association with the business of self-government.

One can make a start toward extricating oneself from political anonymity by concentrating one's first attentions on electing key policy makers. This obviously requires knowledge of the structure of government and the requirements of offices to be filled, as well as the qualifications of the competing candidates. Personality factors must be weighed along with job specifications, for it takes many-dimensional political calipers to select well-fitting pegs for political holes. The major key to elections is in the calibre of the men who have been selected to run against each other.

Unfortunately, when citizens ignore the nominating process, the ballot may offer little better than a choice among evils. It may then be a kind of grab bag; you mark your X and you take your chances. As we have seen, the realities behind political battles are often hidden below the surface of election day activities. But whether open and aboveboard or hidden and devious, the process of selecting nominees is basic to democratic government. This fact should make the primary election of paramount importance to every citizen-politician.

A citizen going to the polls has a big job on his hands. He has to satisfy his conscience that his vote is wise and informed, and he wants to feel that it is influential. The more he knows about the political process, the more he becomes aware that the ballot is only the most obvious feature of the selection process. And the more he knows, the less content he will be to choose from a stable of party stalwarts, to follow the directions of party leaders. He will feel impelled to take a hand in the process; at which point his rewards and his challenges start multiplying in a satisfying fashion.

We have pointed out that the obvious way to make one's full weight felt is inside one or the other of the great parties, for the political independent can at best exercise only external pressures. Unless he is eligible to vote in a party primary, his independence may result in a forfeit of his right to participate in the selection of the election slate. All he can then do is complain. To be successful any independent movement has to become a kind of a political party itself; it always takes an organization to beat an organization. Thus whether an individual chooses to work inside or outside the parties, he needs intimate understanding of nominating and electing procedures, of party structure and operations and of capacities of candidates.

Conscientious would-be voters are often frustrated by the lack of knowledge on which to base an intelligent vote. However in many communities there are civic groups who make it an important part of their business to compile and distribute the kinds of information which voters badly need. Of course such information is often slanted to fit the interests of the collecting group, but it is not too difficult to sift the wheat of useful unbiased information from the chaff of blatant propaganda. To learn to do such sieving is a first responsibility for any citizen-politician.

The most widely available election information is that published in the newspapers and disseminated by radio and television. Such information may or may not be free from partisanship, but usually an earnest inquirer can learn to detect such a bias. Most newspapers print sample ballots conspicuously marked to show the journal's editorial endorsement. A little sustained attention to the editorial columns of the paper will soon reveal its political leanings. But even here there is a problem. For example, the Democrats say that two-thirds of the papers have editorial policies which generally favor Republicans, but the Republicans counter by contending that many of the writers and columnists give a Democratic slant. Despite these claims and counter-claims, one can get much help from the newspapers in getting election information. In fact, the papers are invaluable sources of election information. They are particularly useful in local elections, where it is often hardest to get information.

Candidates' records are summarized and published by many organizations. Usually these also are selective in terms of the special interests of the publishing organization. But even so they are revealing and, if used with discretion, an invaluable source of voter information. The League of Women Voters, which is staunchly nonpartisan, has made a major contribution through its printed candidates' records and its tabulations of candidates' answers to key questions. Labor, farm, and industrial organizations and most so-called independent voters' groups also make extensive use of candidates' records. Most of these have their own axes to grind, and their output must be carefully evaluated. With this sort of treatment, valuable nuggets of information can be sifted out. And into any voter's hopper will go the publications and the exhortations of the parties, their workers, and their candidates. The recommendations of groups like bar associations, taxpayer and other civic associations are often informative and valuable.

Many citizen-politicians find it helpful to take their own marked ballots to the polling places with them. With a little effort it is possible, in the weeks before election, to make a collection of the sorts of voter information described here, and in the last hours before decision to distill the information onto a sample ballot that reflects an informed point of view. Of course such attempts have to stand firm against the blandishments of propaganda blasts that may have little or no civic substance. All of this adds up to the fact that an alert and determined citizen can, if he wants, find out enough about candidates, propositions, and issues to make sensible decisions.

Part of any voter's problem, these days, is the number of offices to be filled and the number of propositions on which he must pass judgment. Also voters are frequently uncertain as to the responsibilities and the requirements of many of the offices. But over years of civic participation, as knowledge of the structure and operation of government and of the parties keeps growing, a feel for job specifications emerges and voter choices become more and more meaningful. Each time the process gets a little easier.

It is obvious, however, that the voter's task could, and should, be made more manageable. Shorter ballots, clearer statements concerning the propositions, better publicity concerning government and party organization and candidates would make the voters' choices easier. Then perhaps more voters would make the effort of voting; at least they would have less excuse for failing to inform themselves before they face the ballot box.

In this connection, the alert citizen-politician should remember that there has to be a balance between his desires to participate directly in decision-making and his confusion over the size and complexity of the ballot. Effective control of policy is not necessarily directly correlated with getting more and more issues directly before the public for a vote. Oftentimes well-meaning citizens press for expanded initiative and referendum provisions, thinking they are taking control away from the professionals, when in fact by cluttering up the ballot they may actually be making it easier for a machine or group to control elections. Modern-day issues are becoming so complex that it becomes ever more difficult to explain them briefly and simply, as should be done to get an intelligent referendum on them. Anyone who has been a legislator or prepared legislation for consideration will attest to the complexity of many issues today; a conscientious legislator must spend many hours studying and poring over proposed bills.

THE VOTING PROCESS AND THE PUBLIC INTEREST

To the ordinary citizen-politician, the mysteries of elections are many, and not all of them are on the ballot itself. Even the rules of the game vary widely, from state to state and from community to community, while the machinations of professional politicians can make steady heads swim. Small wonder that citizen-politicians often feel lost before they start; and yet, there *is* a kind of pattern behind the excitement and confusion of elections.

When a few score neighbors and friends gather together in a typical New England town meeting the process of selecting officials and deciding issues is not difficult. But the rapidly growing needs of government have made it increasingly necessary to rely on representative government, and the selection of these representatives has come to demand greater formality. Questions such as these are always difficult: Who can vote? How can the voting lists be kept up to date? How are the ballots to be counted? Who is to run the election machinery? Who will pay the expenses? Who decides what goes on the ballot? How much direction are successful candidates to have, and by whom, after election?

The regulation of election procedures

Election procedures have gone through many changes and are widely different in different jurisdictions; even qualifications for voting vary greatly. In two states qualified persons eighteen or over may vote; but in most states the legal gateway to voting citizenship is twenty-one. Generally, residence requirements (in state, county, or precinct) are rigidly prescribed. It used to be that whole blocks of citizens were barred from voting: non-property owners, women, and Negroes. But such restrictions are being lifted, one by one. The voting rights of women and Negroes in national election are now guaranteed by constitutional amendment (though in practice Negroes in some areas have many hurdles before they can vote, as was still apparent in the 1956 election). Today nine out of ten adults are eligible to vote. This is an almost complete reversal of the situation in 1790, when only one out of ten could vote.

The formal registration of eligible voters is relatively new. It has been made increasingly necessary by population growth, increasing mobility of people, and increasing impersonality of urban living. Every state prescribes some method of listing voters; some employ a kind of voting census, others require personal registration at prescribed intervals. In an increasing number of states permanent registration is now in effect. This device allows a properly registered voter to retain his right to vote unless he moves out of the jurisdiction or otherwise changes his legal status.

Other facets of the voting process are also regulated. The form of ballot and tallying regulations are generally spelled out in detail. The Australian, or secret, ballot was first introduced into this country late in the nineteenth century, and before that time candidates (or the parties) printed and distributed ballots. Such procedures were obviously open to widespread abuse, and governments now generally print official ballots at public expense. They also provide for the handling of the ballots and counting the vote. Fifteen states use the so-called "Massachusetts ballot," which groups candidates by office, with or without party labels. The "Indiana" or party-type ballot assigns a column to each party; its name or emblem usually appears at the top and there is a party box in which an X casts a vote for the entire party slate. (This cannot be done on the Massachusetts ballot.) In the states that have adopted voting machines, candidates may be grouped in the same way as on a paper ballot, a party lever taking the place of a party box.

The regulations governing what candidates and what propositions may appear on the ballots vary as widely as voting procedures, depending on state constitutional and legislative enactments. The federal nature of our government leaves wide leeway for such local variations.

Even absentee voting raises problems. Many states now allow servicemen to vote, but not long ago this was not the case. A few states are experimenting with the shut-in vote, which allows crippled or ill persons who cannot get to the polls to cast a vote. And most states have some provision for allowing qualified voters to cast a ballot away from home or before leaving the state if the voter knows he will be away on election day. Government employees working in Washington are among those who are allowed to cast absentee ballots in most states. As graphic evidence of the variety of regulations, the Washington newspapers periodically carry a series of columns describing various state absentee ballot requirements.

To demonstrate still another complicated facet of this problem, the State of Rhode Island in 1956 first thought it had elected its incumbent Democratic governor, Dennis J. Roberts, when the regular ballots were counted, only to find that the Republican, Christopher Del Sesto, was declared the winner after the absentee ballots, including those of servicemen, were tabulated. This decision was challenged in the courts, in part on the grounds that the state absentee voter law was illegal. The Democrats contended that at least several absentee voters had died before election day, but that their votes had been counted none the less. On January 1, 1957, the courts decided against the inclusion of some six thousand absentee ballots, with the result that the Democratic incumbent was the winner of this on-again-off-again contest after all.

The 1947 aldermanic contest in Chicago involved one of the authors in an interesting legal test of the voting laws brought by his unsuccessful opponent. The Illinois law says that an aldermanic candidate to be elected must receive more than 50 per cent of the vote. Without this margin, a run-off between the two highest candidates is required. Merriam received slightly over 50 per cent of the counted votes, but less than 50 per cent of all votes cast (a number of ballots having been voided because they were spoiled—improperly marked with a check rather than a cross, with an identifying mark on them, a vote for two candidates, and so forth). The question was whether the law referred to all votes cast or only to those counted as valid ballots. Actually there had been rulings on both sides of this question, but in this instance the court ruled that only valid ballots were to be considered—and Merriam was declared the winner without the necessity of a run-off.

The tallying of election results is always a big job; and the public has a key stake in the honesty of the tally. Counting paper ballots is a long and tedious process. It is carried on at the end of a long hard day; the judges and clerks are tired and mistakes are easy to make. The candidates and the parties have a political-life-and-death stake in the results. And unless the opposition or the public is vigilant the count may be inaccurate or worse.

In recent years voting machines have been introduced to end the drudgery of the hand tally and to minimize mistakes. Machine-voting also reduces certain of the opportunities to tamper with the tally, although no machine is proof against determined vote manipulators (see next section on preventing election frauds). Voting machines involve large capital outlays, but they cut down the working hours of millions of election officials.

Regulations have an important effect on voting and elections. Where the law is too restrictive, for whatever the reasons, otherwise eligible voters may be disfranchised. The American Heritage Foundation, for example, estimated that nearly 10 million eligible voters were unable to cast ballots in the 1956 presidential election because of these legal barriers: about 6 million could not meet residence requirements because they had recently moved; another 800,000 could not meet literacy requirements for specific state registration; and another 500,000 were residents of the District of Columbia, to note the largest categories.

Thus the alert citizen-politician wants to know what his own election laws say, how they could be improved, and if they are being properly administered. Should his state insist on a year's residence before a new resident can vote? Or would six months be fairer? Could there be more adequate provision for absentee voting? Is time off allowed from work to allow a person to vote? Are the hours of voting such as to encourage maximum participation? Is the registration law effective, and is it being enforced (take another look at Chapter One in this regard)? The periods and the commas of what sometimes seems to be a dull and unimportant set of laws and regulations may be the difference between domination by a political machine or incompetents and decent, honest and competent representation. And that difference, in turn, may decide whether your city has an adequate water supply or not, whether your garbage is collected regularly or not, or how long your son spends in the service.

Elections are big business. Our million or more elected officials are selected in hundreds of elections. The election machinery which is now required is enormously expensive. Most states and many metropolitan areas in a presidential election year spend millions of dollars in maintaining election machinery, servicing polling places, printing ballots, and paying election judges and clerks. These costs rise to hundreds of millions of dollars across the nation. To some extent, these large expenditures are unavoidable. But it may well be that they are sometimes needlessly high. Most people will agree that many ballots are much too long, making it almost impossible for citizens to exercise intelligent choices. Candidates may be unknown and even some offices may be unfamiliar. Periodical efforts have been made to reduce the number of elective offices and improve the ballots, but without startling success.

Frauds and their prevention

Human nature being what it is, and politics being a game with high stakes, almost every political novice is likely to come up against activities of doubtful legality. To be forewarned is to be forearmed. The ballot box is an important focus for illegal political operations. The alert citizen-politician needs to learn to read the straws that bend to a corrupt wind when it rises around the polling place.

Most political organizations, even political machines, would prefer not to have to run the risks of tampering with election procedures. But when stakes run high the temptations are great, and few dyed-in-the-wool machines have great qualms about taking a hand to insure favorable results. Since the adoption of the secret ballot, it is not always possible for such machines to be sure that the faithful actually vote as promised. But corrupt politicians, like other people, like to get their money's worth, and they are ingenious in figuring out ways of being sure that the ballot box actually holds the votes that have been promised. Their henchmen, clustering around the polling place, serve as walking reminders of pre-election promises. A great deal of ingenuity has been expended in developing ways of controlling votes. Although state after state has outlawed one election fraud after another, new ones keep popping up and old ones work their way around the edges of the law. Election frauds are of three main sorts: (1) frauds in the enrolling of voters in the file of legal registrants, (2) frauds in voting, and (3) frauds in the counting of votes.

Much legislative attention has been given to working out registration systems so that only legal voters are permitted to vote, but loopholes are persistently punched through all these regulations. Generally, would-be voters are required to register *in person* well in advance of election day and there is usually some sort of check-up to see that the official list really includes persons entitled to vote by reason of age, citizenship, residence, and other qualifications. Such voters are registered either before each election or permanently "until such time as they move away or get married or otherwise change their voting status." Each voter signs a duplicate registration form; one is kept on file in the Board of Elections and the other is in a roster at the local polling place. Signatures can be compared with the names which the voters write on an application form when they receive a ballot on election day.

Permanent registration laws and other regulations have undoubtedly narrowed the areas in which the forces of corruption operate. It is increasingly difficult, for example, for a voter to vote more than once in a given precinct or to cast his vote in precinct after precinct, as "floaters" used to do in the heyday of rough-and-tumble city elections. But even permanent registration is no sure guarantee of an honest election. "Ghost voters"—names that should have been removed from the rolls when their owners moved or died—continue to haunt the polling places as they did in the 1955 Chicago campaign. Such ghosts always carry much more political weight than their ectoplasmic condition would seem to indicate; they generally have strong partisan political leanings. Their behavior is far from random and rarely on the side of a good civic conscience.

Rigged elections do not stop with registration frauds. The voting place is too often the scene of other frauds. The ballots themselves are sometimes tampered with or illegal pressures are put on voters. Chain-voting is sometimes used to start a reaction in favor of candidates sponsored by less than scrupulous interests. It works this way: an official ballot is acquired by hook or by crook. It is carefully marked, and entrusted to a cooperative voter. He also receives his own legal ballot as he enters the voting booth. He disappears behind the curtain, folds up the unmarked ballot, stores it away, pulls out the marked ballot, emerges and deposits it in the ballot box. On leaving the polling place, he proceeds to a predetermined rendezvous where he hands over his own unmarked ballot and pockets his fee, if one has been agreed upon. His ballot is in turn carefully "voted" and turned over to another accomplice. This process can be repeated as long as willing voters hold out. The buyer is thus sure that promised votes are actually delivered. The success of this process obviously depends on obtaining that first unmarked ballot. This requires the cooperation of the official printer, of someone in the office of the election commission, or of the election officials in the polling place.

Sometimes ballots are illegally marked during the count. The "short-pencil" technique has already been described. But with the cynical collusion of election officials the illegal marking of ballots can go on openly and rapidly. When voting machines were introduced, tampering techniques had to be brought up to date. The setting of the machine to produce predetermined results is usually beyond the mechanical ingenuity of the would-be tamperers. But machines can be jammed on purpose, false instructions can be given out, and voters can be intimidated or led to believe that they need assistance in recording their vote on the machine. They can be tricked into voting a straight ticket by being told that they must throw the Democratic or the Republican master lever. The relative newness of voting machines and citizen awe when faced with such machinery for the first time has produced many errors. These along with voter ignorance and timidity are quick to be exploited by corrupt election officials.

The most obvious way to throw an election is the deliberate miscount of ballots. *Close attention* by voter and watcher *is most important* in insuring an honest count. Any mark except a clear and unmistakable X well contained in the square preceding the candidate's name may invalidate a ballot. Ballots can also be discarded for all sorts of other reasons and even the manifest intent of the voter cannot always save them. Interpretation of election regulations can be used to throw deciding votes to preferred candidates. The tally itself can be doctored; a few votes can be added after hours and cross-checking totals altered. Split tickets are especially susceptible to this sort of voting manipulation. It takes collusion to change the count of straight tickets but split tickets are always difficult to tally accurately; and it requires vigilance on the part of a watcher or clerk to be sure that the tally is correct.

Every citizen-politician needs to know enough about election laws to know what his rights are and how to protect them. He needs to know what to do when his registration or vote is challenged and to whom to appeal in suspicious circumstances. A working knowledge of election rules and regulations will stand him in good stead. These are always available from the local Board of Elections, and many civic groups publish supplementary materials which are free of legal verbiage.

Simplifying elections

The public's interest in fair and meaningful elections can be defeated in many perfectly legal ways. Long ballots, covering dozens of minor offices, always give a political machine an advantage, for obviously voting the straight ballot is the easiest way out. Such long ballots are always heavily criticized by those who want to make citizens' choices responsible and meaningful but they are less vigorously condemned by those who stand to gain from public apathy and confusion. The use of legal verbiage to confuse and discourage voters has been notably exploited, particularly in connection with propositions on the ballot. The official wording frequently conceals all substantive meaning behind such phrases as "An Act to Amend line 7, article 51, of Public Law 796." Legal abbreviations, double negatives, and other verbal disguises can also be used to hide meaning. When an organization wants to be sure that a particular proposition passes, it carefully instructs its loyal supporters how to vote, though it may not bother to tell them what the proposition means. It is quite possible, unless newspapers and civic groups are alert, that the general public may, in the isolation of the election booth, meet the proposition for the first time in the form of an incomprehensible abstraction.

The position to which a proposition or even a candidate is assigned on a ballot is important; the upper-left-hand corner has a reading advantage over any other position. Type style and size are also important. All such factors can be manipulated to defeat the public interest and the citizen-politician needs to be alert to every trick of a black trade that would prevent a vote from truly reflecting the wishes of the electorate.

Many of the reform measures around which civic groups have rallied deal with one aspect or another of the voting process. There is no doubt that such devices as the voting machine, permanent registration, and the short ballot have all made contributions to honest elections. But no one of them, nor all of them together, can turn the whole trick. Election irregularities are still with us, and citizen apathy can often be traced in part to cynicism concerning the honesty of elections. Even honestly conducted elections can arouse frustration and then apathy if the ballots are of bed-sheet proportions. There is need for continuous restructuring of the election process so that private citizens can make meaningful selections. Regulations need further streamlining so that voters need not stumble over technicalities which obscure the real issues.

THE CITIZEN-POLITICIAN IN THE POLLING PLACE

Since the voting booth stands at the nexus of the democratic process, the citizen-politician needs to make sure that the procedures that surround it are above suspicion. Serving at the polling place on election day is the best way to start. It is not hard to find an opportunity to serve. Many organizations recruit and train watchers and other election personnel to supplement and to check on party workers. Volunteer watchers and judges and clerks of election are much sought after. Aside from the satisfactions of doing one's civic duty, such assignments are valuable political education. Judges and clerks, unlike the watchers, are usually paid a small per diem fee, and they are usually formally endorsed by party officials.

If you want to be a watcher notify your candidate's headquarters or your local precinct captain. You will be given credentials and instructed as to what to watch for and what to do if your suspicions are aroused. It is always good practice to familiarize yourself in advance with the official regulations and to appear armed with a copy. Insist on calling the local Board of Elections if you are in doubt. Appeal to the local police if necessary; in many places a policeman is assigned to every polling place.

Check each voter off on the official precinct list as he votes. This will help prevent duplicate voting. It will also help other precinct workers earmark laggard votes so that they can be corralled before closing time.

If you are a watcher during the count of a paper ballot, a real job is cut out for you. And again familiarity with the regulations is important. In almost every precinct the following sorts of problems will arise:

Spoiled ballots;

Illegally marked ballots (such as a check mark instead of an X, or a mark outside the square in front of the candidate's name);

Absentee ballots which may need special validation;

Split ballots where the voter clearly intends *not* to vote a straight ticket (for example a mark in the party circle at the top of the column, and also marks for individual candidates in the opposing column).

The job of the watcher is not done until all the ballots are in the hands of the authorized election officials at central headquarters. Also the final tally should be duly reported to the proper party as well as public officials. Until the last "i" is dotted it is still possible for unscrupulous persons to doctor the tally.

When these final tasks are done the volunteer watcher may leave with the feeling that his civic duty has been well done. No one who has so served will ever neglect to vote in subsequent elections, and he will vote with care. And he is not likely to rest on his laurels; he is probably in politics to stay. His initiation as a guardian of the ballot box will dig itself deeply into his civic attitudes.

CHAPTER SIX

Professionalism and Politics

PROFESSIONALISM AND THE PUBLIC SERVICE

Political appointments and the merit system

Election victories carry with them the ultimate responsibility for post-election political appointments. This power of appointment is one of the powerful magnets that draw out the tremendous effort which parties and candidates put forth. The total of the appointive offices which the successful party controls is a major factor in party calculations. But it is also a matter of grave public concern, since it influences the calibre of government administration. As we have noted, the spoils system was inaugurated in the Jacksonian era. The "spoils" in question were jobs on the public payroll, and Jacksonian Democrats soon moved into them in swarms. This started some fifty years of undismayed gorging at the public trough, but eventually the public became restive. When a disappointed office seeker shot President Garfield the nation decided that it was "time for a change," and the first United States Civil Service Act was passed. Since then the merit system has spread unevenly but, in spite of occasional backsliding, steadily.

Today, over 90 per cent of all employees of the national

government are under civil service. However, administrators at every level of government still retain a measure of administrative discretion in picking personnel. The merit system provides that their selections must be made on the basis of demonstrated qualifications. Generally, appointees must be selected from a roster of persons who have passed civil service examinations. Civil service appointments carry with them certain rights of tenure, including protection against irresponsible firings for political or other reasons. But key government positions such as cabinet, subcabinet, and high policy posts still remain as political appointments on the theory that such policy-forming positions should reflect the election mandate. The line separating civil service from policy appointments is elastic, and is always subject to redefinition after a change in party fortunes.

The merit system has spread more slowly to local and state governments; as yet nearly two-thirds of such local governments have no merit system. The spoils system has always flourished with special lushness at the local level, for the contacts between special interests and public officials are closer and more frequent. There are also more regulations, regulatory bodies, and licensing bodies which some private businesses feel as harassments that they would gladly pay to be rid of. And unhappily the prestige of many state and local governments is lower. Whatever the reasons, it is a recognized fact that, while abuses are diminishing, some city halls, county courthouses, and state capitols are still market places for extra-legal (if not illegal) political favors. One observer of this state of affairs commented that "folks seem to be born with built-in insulation against local and state scandals."

Both ideological and grimly practical battles rage back and forth over political appointments. For three generations, at least, this issue has been in the spotlight. It is a complicated one. There is much force to the argument that most, if not all, the public service should be divorced from the pressures of party politics. Certainly a stable, independent, self-respecting civil service can provide both expertness and continuity to governmental operations. It has succeeded notably in Great Britain, building the kind of professionalism that puts loyalty to the job above loyalty to a party. Such reasoning animates the drive for the extension of the merit system.

But the merit system is not without critics. It has produced cumbersome rigidities and, some say, so much security on the job that it fosters a shovel-leaning approach to public employment. The difficulties of organizing millions of public employees in a workable, flexible, civil service system are enormous; and it is small wonder that the process often fails to keep up with the fast-moving pace of government operation. Critics also point out that a rigid system hamstrings necessary administrative discretion. The task of tying such administrative discretion to a personnel system which provides for competence, justice, and stability is difficult. Appointive policy-making jobs are defended on the ground that the administrator must be able to build a harmonious, working team, but the line which divides policy jobs from non-policy jobs is never easily established and never constant. Sometimes it is shifted for good administrative reasons, but sometimes it is moved to fit the job lust of the party in power.

It is strongly argued that the winning party must be able to control the over-all direction of government if it is to function as a responsible agent of the majority. Few will deny the general validity of this argument, but there is, again, little agreement as to the point at which to draw the line between the political and the nonpolitical decision. Despite howls of anguish from old-time party henchmen, the general trend is toward a broadened merit system; the nation's clear intent is to build up professional competence in the public services. The effectiveness of any civil service law, however, depends on the personnel which is charged with its administration.

Party regulars frequently have little enthusiasm for tightly administered civil service laws and spend much effort looking for loopholes through which to insert their supporters. A favorite device is to hire "temporaries." These persons generally are not required to meet rigid civil service requirements, and such temporary appointments are defended on the grounds that they offer administrators the necessary latitude to meet unusual situations, emergencies, or peak loads. But a hidden and large increase in the number of temporaries generally means that a spoilsman has his finger in the jam pot. At one time Chicago, to its shame, had thousands of temporary teachers regularly employed in the school system. It took concentrated civic indignation to work out procedures which would insulate the superintendent of schools from the partisan pressures which had brought this about. When that was accomplished, the Chicago public schools miraculously found that in spite of growing enrollments they could get along with relatively few temporaries.

The problem of blending professional competence with party responsibility is a major challenge to democratic procedures, and progress is being made in a seesaw fashion. When a spoils system becomes too flagrant, it is countered by broadening public support for civil service standards and procedures. Similarly, when civil service procedures become ensnarled in bureaucratic red tape it becomes time to resurvey all aspects of this problem. These are matters in which everyone is involved, the individual citizen as well as the parties and the public servants.

In any event, the expansion of the merit system has led to greater demands for qualified career employees. A wide range of expertness is needed for the many facets of government activity. And more and more positions are crying for, searching for, and finding qualified persons who have been trained for the job.

Career jobs are largely limited to the executive branch of

government. Judicial appointments, of course, involve a highly
specialized kind of expertness, and the number of nonjudicial
positions in the judicial branch is limited. Legislative bodies
are daily expanding their staffs of expert assistants: legislative
draftsmen, reference service personnel, and committee staffs
all fall into this category. But the number of positions in these
areas is limited, and most of them are filled from the ranks of
those qualified for or working in corresponding executive
branch agencies.

The use of examinations to qualify individuals for government jobs continues to rise rapidly. In the national government actually fewer than five thousand jobs changed hands
when the Republicans took over from the Democrats in 1952
(much to the distress of many Republican party professionals). Progressive personnel officers in government now go
out to "sell" their programs to promising recruits just as business firms do. Colleges, of course, are a fertile source of
government workers of the future, but all kinds of skills are
needed. In the municipal field, the rapid growth of the city
manager system has created a brand new career service in
government, for which many individuals are now specifically
trained. Many city managers hire assistants who will in turn
become the technical administrators that direct the day-by-
day affairs of the city.

Government service in a well-run branch of the public service has much to offer. Every year we are becoming more
aware of the necessity to attract competent persons to government service, and the incentives are being developed to compete with other types of opportunity. While the government
employee, at least beyond a certain median level, will never
receive the financial reward that business affords, the fringe
benefits may be greater, including liberal leave and sickness
allowances, opportunities for good retirement benefits, and
job protection through the merit system.

Rising standards of professionalism

Another indication of increasing professionalization of the government service is the growing size and prestige of professional organizations in the public services—organizations such as the American Society for Public Administration, the National Association of Assessing Officials, the International City Managers Association, the National Association of Housing and Redevelopment Officials, the American Society of Planning Officials, the American Public Works Association, the American Public Welfare Association, the American Public Health Association, the Federation of Tax Administrators, the Municipal Finance Officers Association, the International Association of Chiefs of Police and the companion organization of firemen, the Public Personnel Association, and so on. These are private professional organizations whose overriding purposes are to provide clearance of information, to encourage improvement and standardization of procedures, and to professionalize the public services. Such associations are doing much to build up prestige and the competence of public administration. One cluster of such organizations in Chicago, originally brought together by the Public Administration Clearing House, reaches some 100,000 public officials, making important contributions to the businesslike handling of the public's business.

Along with the development of specialties a broader science of public administration has grown up. Its purpose is to integrate specialized operations into sound administrative units. To meet the danger that overspecialization can fracture the whole, increasing emphasis is currently being put on the role of the administrative generalist—the administrator who sees things topside. The city manager profession takes this approach to the complicated problems of city government, and at the national level important integrative functions have been made the responsibility of the Bureau of the Budget.

The problem of harnessing the sprawling complexity of modern government has been the subject of recommendations by a number of commissions set up by presidential or gubernatorial directive. The President's Committee on Administrative Management, the two Hoover Commissions on Government Reorganization, and the President's Committee on Intergovernmental Relations are some of the best known. They have concerned themselves not only with the functioning of special departments but with the knotty problem of over-all integration. The commission approach is also being tried out at state and municipal levels, but too often on a timid and piecemeal basis.

The future of democratic government depends on our ability to harness specialized professionalism to the over-all requirements of huge governmental responsibilities. The success or failure of this effort depends on political parties as much as it does on the professions and the civil service. Policy makers, wherever they are—in political parties, in pressure groups, or in government—stand at the center of this process. It is imperative that citizens in and out of the parties give their representatives appropriate authority as well as a clear mandate to keep this huge business of government working at maximum efficiency. If public offices are to be manned by dedicated public servants and not simply by party hacks, the parties must find other sources of support than payrollers. Citizen-politicians will have to come forward to do the party jobs if democratic government is truly to work for all the people.

The parties naturally take special interest in the millions of jobs which the three levels of government represent. It takes 7 million civilian employees (in addition to the 1 million-plus elected officials) to run the more than 100,000 governmental units. Together with their families such employees constitute a major segment of our population. Most of these persons are aware of their direct stake in government; and blocs of vested

interests keep coalescing. There is always a threat of bureaucratic strangulation when so large a group has a stake in
things-as-they-are. Rigidities and red tape tend to grow like
Penelope's web. They have to be determinedly unraveled if
they are not to handicap the free growth of democratic institutions.

The rest of us also have a major stake in the network of
governments, if only as taxpayers and as recipients of government services. The public interest must transcend that of
the officeholder. By a variety of devices, civil service laws,
Hatch acts, antistrike laws, and so forth, we keep trying to
prevent the public services from hardening into power blocs
that can take advantage of a monopoly position. This is a
never finished task. Even when many government jobs are
filled by civil service procedures—and thus partially cushioned
against political raiding—ultimate control resides finally in the
hands of elected officials. These in turn depend heavily on
party support. No matter what safeguards are erected around
particular jobs, in a democracy government operations are
ultimately political and thus subject to the close attention of
both parties. The public should certainly be equally concerned.

The party out of office will always make election capital
out of the "dangers of an intrenched, self-seeking bureauc-
racy." Both parties naturally beat the drums for "government
reorganization," "economy," "honest, efficient government,"
"an end to corruption and graft." The "new broom," "the
clean sweep," "time for a change," always have great political
appeal. The issue of efficient government offers inexhaustible
grist for campaign mills. And if such slogans represent something more than campaign fodder they make an important
contribution to democratic government. The thorough ventilation of the problems of government administration is one of
the important contributions that political parties can make.

PROFESSIONALISM AND PARTY POLITICS

Politics is people

One of the reasons there are no colleges or even correspondence schools for politicians is that politics is people. The professional politician is a specialist in people and in human relationships. It is part of democracy's creed that he must win by persuasion, not by intimidation or bribery. He has to be able to enlist cooperation even under circumstances that may not be immediately rewarding. To build an organization he has to be able to persuade some persons to be followers and others to be leaders.

Personal—human—relationships are the essence of any organization. Their importance is attested by the attention which is currently being directed to the sciences of human relations. Political organizations are under special pressure to work out rewarding personal relationships, for politics deals extensively in intangibles. Position, salary, prestige, influence, dreams of a political future—yes, and of distinguished public service—are all involved, and these cannot be neatly totaled up in some incentive scheme. Just as there are no formulas which will forecast elections with certainty, so there are none for building political organizations; political pleasures, as well as pains, are too tightly tied to personal factors.

The personal equation, which no good politician ignores, is one of the basic resources of democratic government. Democracy both in theory and practice builds on the uniqueness of personality, on the dignity of *persons as persons*. People are its main resource and its strength, just as their welfare is its chief goal. They become personally committed to democracy as to no other form of government.

The dedicated citizen-politician, with an aptitude for working with people, functions well within the context of democratic institutions. He helps to weld like-thinking citizens into an organization which can influence even when it cannot totally control government. But obviously this is no task for itinerant amateurs. Winning friends and influencing voters is more than a once-or-twice-a-year job. While politicians may also be good lawyers, economists, farmers, businessmen, or labor leaders, none of these skills alone will make a good politician. Persuasion, leadership—even educated followership —needs the reinforcement of political understanding which can come only through participation. The skillful politician learns to blend vital political ingredients with an artistry that takes account of the essential fluidity of the political situation. Each new day, sometimes each new hour, radically changes the political picture, and it takes a professional touch to manage political improvisation. The practiced amateur as well as the professional develops an ability to listen with a third, fourth, or even fifth ear. He learns to roll with the punch, to change his tack and even his goals as the political winds shift.

The "training" of a politician

Professionalism in the public service is not the same thing as professionalism in politics, though the two may on occasion merge. Training of party professionals is largely self-education. It grows as chores are done, as problems emerge and are handled, as contacts with the old professionals and new civic pressures unfold. Little systematic instruction is available to speed the learning process. The Reeds, in the study on *Preparing College Men and Women for Politics* sponsored by the Citizenship Clearing House, pointed out the paucity of formal political training at the college level.[1] Civics courses in secondary schools are even thinner. There is scarcely a suggestion that students might some day become either amateur or professional politicians, or indeed that democracy demands such participation by citizens in large numbers.

[1] Thomas H. Reed and Doris D. Reed, *Preparing College Men and Women for Politics,* A report to the citizenship Clearing House affiliated with the law center of New York University (New York, 1952).

The parties themselves have begun to undertake some systematic training of volunteers. Both parties have sporadically produced sheaves of training manuals and training films for canvassers and poll watchers. Both run political schools for party members at various levels all the way up to the national committeemen. This sort of education is on the increase. The more enterprising of the independent political groups such as the Americans for Democratic Action have been active in this field, and the League of Women Voters is justly famous for its able literature on public issues and government operations. Get-out-the-vote campaigns are systematically organized within and without the parties. Service and civic groups, as well as special interests, join in this effort. The chambers of commerce (particularly the junior chambers of commerce), the great trade unions, and the leading farm groups all work at recruiting poll watchers, registration and get-out-the-vote campaigns, and so forth. Many organizations conduct workshops. The Citizens-for-Merriam devoted much time and effort to such grass root instruction.

Any citizen who wants an education in political action should look for such "schools" in his area. If they are lacking he may be able to find an experienced group—partisan or not —that is willing to take on such a project. Such training is only a start, albeit an important start, in the education of the citizen-politician. The next steps in political education must often be taken without benefit of instruction, though the old pro's, like most people, are fond of giving advice. The willing learner can learn rapidly but in the final analysis he will have to chart his own map of the strange and bewildering world of personal political pressures.

One helpful tool is a firm grounding in parliamentary procedures. Political action sooner or later becomes group action, and orderly procedures for handling public debates and for resolving conflicts play an important part in crystallizing democratic decisions. The political impact of parliamentary procedures is, however, two-edged. They can help to organize action or to obstruct the efforts of the opposition. Parliamentary tricks have often defeated legislative action, and marathon talkathons—filibusters—perennially make headlines on Capitol Hill. Both are a direct outgrowth of the procedures designed to protect the right of unlimited debate, but they are often used by minorities to prevent majorities from winning their rightful decision. Although filibusters are much criticized as obstructionist, the issue of the right to be heard is important. Generally accepted procedures are necessary in crystallizing majority consent. Citizen-politicians will better understand what is going on in legislatures and conventions and will be more skillful in lining up support or in preventing railroading through of measures if they have a working knowledge of parliamentary procedures and of the special rules which such bodies impose on themselves. Roberts' *Rules of Order* is a veritable bible for group leaders and politicians.

Politicians, professional as well as amateur, come from every walk of life, but it is scarcely surprising that many of them are lawyers. This is true in all legislatures, from the city council to the Congress of the United States. In the Eighty-fifth Congress, for example, 65 per cent of the Senators and 56 per cent of the Representatives are lawyers. Other professions of members in order of predominance are: business or banking, agriculture, teaching, journalism, and the medical and engineering professions. Engineers, accountants, and so forth, are also well represented, and there are always smatterings of businessmen, farmers, and labor leaders in all legislatures. Politics is becoming more and more a full-time job, although the lower rungs are usually not profitable enough for men to cut themselves completely loose from other sources of income.

Many professional politicians have government jobs. Although the merit system is making inroads on this practice, the pattern is far from broken. A large proportion of precinct captains, many local committeemen, and even some higher officials of the parties often hold simultaneous jobs in government. The citizen-politician needs to be alert to the backgrounds and the business connections of the professionals if he is to make sensible judgments as to their disinterestedness, competence, and integrity.

The public's stake in the private morality of public figures is enormous. Well-known political figures like Senator Paul Douglas of Illinois have pointed out that in democratic government public servants owe a special duty of private and public integrity. They should lean over backwards to avoid profiting from their privileged position. Scandals about the five percenters who traded their knowledge of the Washington merry-go-round for a share in the dollar value of the government contracts which they helped engineer did much to focus public attention on this issue. Obviously, the private lives of the professionals have much pertinence in judging their suitability as well as their competence for public office.

Public office: headaches and rewards

The ardors of campaigning set forth in Chapter One may well tempt you to ask, "Why would anyone want elective office at such a price?" The answer is not easy or always logical.

There is no denying that running for public office is costly in time, energy, and money. The candidate keeps paying over and over again in exhaustion, in outraged sensibilities, in the wear and tear on family and friends; and for every winner there is a loser.

The public attitude toward public office is mixed; and most holders of elective office suffer from this ambivalence. Slanderous labels are easily and freely bestowed and the profession of politician is too often smeared with the taint of distrust.

Working conditions in public office also often leave much to be desired. Take the state legislators for example. It is a rare state that pays them more than meagerly. Since most salaries do not adequately support the legislators, and since their expenses are often heavy by reason of dual residences and campaigning, most legislators (unless they are men of private means) are virtually forced to give something less than their full attention to public business. This state of affairs has been defended on the grounds that legislating is not a full-time job because legislatures do not sit around the calendar. This is an extraordinary rationalization when you consider the volume of work that legislatures leave undone and the importance of legislative bodies to the well-being of political democracy.

Most legislators receive certain fringe benefits, but these do not always take the form of sick leave, paid vacation, pensions, and so forth, which the civil servant has come to expect. More likely a special allowance for clerical or other help, or some other special services such as printing, mailing, legislative reference services, may be provided free or at cost. Some states do not provide offices for their legislators, or even desks; there are instances where the rotunda of the state capitol building is the legislator's only office away from home. The Council of State Governments' studies of salaries and perquisites of state legislators make one marvel that the level of legislative activity is as high as it is.

Why then does anyone ever seek public office? The salary, of course, may still be a factor, even though by nonpolitical standards it is rarely large enough to compensate for the exhausting race of a major election. Not only in state and local governments are salaries low; even in the national government they generally run below those of comparable occupations in private industry (except in the lower ranks of the civil service —clerks, business machine operators, typists, and stenographers).

Only at the top of the national government, in the presidency, does a man receive anything like as much as he could command in the market place. Our President now receives a salary of $100,000 plus $50,000 in expenses, $40,000 for travel and entertainment, plus the use of the White House, limousines, a yacht, airplanes, and other fringe benefits. The men below him, even the cabinet officials, do not do nearly as well. They get $25,000, yet their jobs compare in responsibility with those of heads of great corporations who may be paid upwards of $100,000 a year. In the federal civil service there are a few hundred persons who receive $15,000 or more; $12,000 to $15,000 is generally the top rate paid to administrators and key professionals. The top civil service salary is $16,000. Salaries $20,000 or above go to political appointees, cabinet heads, ambassadors, and so forth.

The public service offers intangible rewards, however, that play important roles in the calculations of candidates, public employees, and the parties that sponsor them. Otherwise, men would not fight for the jobs. The powerful inducements are often of the kind that do not get into the statistics. The fringe benefits that exercise hypnotic lure are those that feed ambition for power, for prestige, and for public service. The hopeful and exciting part of this story is how often the last of these, the will to dedicated public service, plays the major role in the personal calculations of politicians. These men see their job as a privilege, and their rewards in the satisfaction of a job well done.

Sometimes too the candidate seeks the approbation of history and of his fellow men. The desire to win a glowing niche in his country's Hall of Fame is not restricted to Presidents in their last terms of office, although they are conspicuously subject to it. Despite the fact that the dignity of the public service has been seriously eroded by open scandal as well as by some mishandled investigations of subversion and alleged subversion, there are still large areas of the public service that carry prestige. Not only Presidents, but Senators, Supreme Court Justices, cabinet officers, and ambassadors occupy posts that the public honors and respects. And if offices further down the scale do not automatically bring prestige, they have been known to acquire it when the officeholder wore his robes with distinction.

The lure of power is a compelling force in politics. This heady stuff is the stock in trade of politicians, and even money can be translated into power terms; candidates often run for election in order to rule. Personal prestige, influence, a place in the political scheme of things, are tempting stakes. Even small-fry politicians find that to be "in the know" is vicariously to be a power, and that the shine of reflected glory can be warming indeed.

The restoration of the good reputation of politics is still part of the great unfinished business of popular government—American style. The name of politics is still suffering from the blackening it received in the heyday of the callous, power-hungry political machine. And every public scandal puts high barriers in the way of its slow upward climb to public approval. It is one of the paradoxes of our great democracy that we still too often look down our noses at the men and women whose vocation is service to democratic government. Yet for many politicians and public officeholders politics and government service are the high calling they deserve to be. In fact, the level of competence, of dedication, of self-sacrifice is much higher than the public credits.

You want to run for office?

Fortunately, despite all obstacles, candidates do turn up in contests for the one million-plus elective offices. Not all are spirited battles, but there are enough close contests every year to make things interesting—and healthy for the future of democracy. But running for office is not a career for which one can train and educate himself—at least not specifically.

Candidates for public office are as varied as are the many kinds of interest and background which make up our country. But even for the "professional" politician there is hardly such a thing as a career in elective office. How, then, does one go about making himself available for public office?

First, there are a few qualifications which we would recommend for potential office-seekers:

1. Don't be thin-skinned.
2. It helps if you like people.
3. The more you know about the processes of government the better.
4. You ought to be acquainted with politicians, and preferably have worked with them in other campaigns.
5. It is easiest if you have the kind of job in which your time is somewhat flexible.

Too many people want to enter the political world at the top. They finally get interested in politics, and want to run for office. They think they are well-qualified (and perhaps they are), and then offer themselves for a congressional nomination, or the like. Many become disillusioned when they are by-passed for someone they consider less qualified. This is a perennial problem at all levels of politics. Such individuals should remember that elective office is in one sense the zenith of political activity, a goal which many people seek after working their way up the ladder of party organization. If it were otherwise it would be just like those business, labor, or professional organizations which fill their top spots from the outside. The morale of any organization soon suffers if the opportunities for in-service promotion are cut off. This is especially true of politics, where the rank and file strongly resent the outsider. The approved way to start is to get into a political organization and do some of the "dirty work" before seeking nomination for office. There have been notable exceptions to this rule, but many otherwise well-qualified citizens have failed to be nominated because they ignored this basic fact of political life. For example, in the Eighty-fifth Congress only 2 per cent of the Senators and 7 per cent of the Representatives had no previous experience in politics.

Some who have overcome these obstacles, and have been elected to office, have not functioned well because they view their new job in a vacuum, without knowledge of either the basic processes of democratic action or public decision-making. Politics and government have some of the qualities of a social science, but the product with which one deals is people and human nature. It is not like selling a product across a counter. And it is not as simple as most other decision-making. Many complex considerations are involved in every political decision.

Officeholders live in a goldfish bowl. Matters which would go unnoticed in almost any other area of activity are subject to public scrutiny and comment. One must accept this fact if he is to present himself for office, at least if he wants peace of mind. An office-holder can be—and often is—criticized for the very things which his critics would do in private without a second thought. But we should not expect things to be otherwise since political activity is the summation of all our collective interests.

Our form of government and its complexities today demand the best possible candidates for public office. It has become increasingly important for unselfish citizens to undertake political party work: as precinct officials, as judges and clerks of election, as campaign workers, as fund raisers, or as party officials. If these jobs are held by those who are concerned first of all with the public welfare it will be easier to secure well-qualified and acceptable candidates.

One last word of advice: you had better find out all the details concerning qualifications for office in your state or community before you make the plunge. You have to be thirty-five or over if you are going to start at the top, as did Wendell Willkie and Dwight Eisenhower, and make your first elective race as a presidential candidate. And you must be at least thirty to run for the Senate. If you are content to start a little lower on the ladder, you still will find certain residence, age, and other requirements which condition your availability. And if you have spent any time on Alcatraz, other than as visitor or employee, you really have a problem.

How Not to Work in Politics:
The Seamier Side

Unfortunately, politics is not yet free of evil influences. While we are anxious to put popular prejudices against politics and politicians in a more realistic perspective, we also believe that the citizen-politician should be aware of some of the corrosive political forces which have been at work in the past, are still in existence in scattered places, and are always lying dormant, waiting only for citizen complacency to rear its head.

What follows is not as typical of politics today as it once was, but it could be if every citizen is not careful.

The powers of the parties can be great, and they present a constant temptation to the ambitious. Political organizations all too easily become self-seeking vested interests. This is characteristic of corrupt political machines. A party organization enchained to bossism can hardly fail to become narcissistic and grasping. Once this happens, its organic unity and power is diverted from public purposes to private interests. Party organization paradoxically is always pulled in two directions: there are pressures working to keep it open-ended and responsive to the membership, but it is also subjected to constant pressure from cliques thirsting for power. The public must be alert and resourceful if it is to be a match for forces which take an intense if nearsighted view of political power. The history of party politics provides abundant evidence to support that familiar axiom: "All power corrupts, and absolute power corrupts absolutely." Danger is strongly present when any private group holds unchallenged the reins of government. The citizen-politician must mount guard against such influence—and his first task is to recognize danger signs.

When a machine takes over

It is no coincidence that boss-ridden machines have functioned best in local governments, especially in municipal government. Such machines are built and maintained through intimate personal contacts. They require organization and pressure to keep them nourished, disciplined, and direct. There have been county bosses and county political machines, state bosses and state political machines, but few of these could match the power or the venality of the big city machines.

Almost every great city at some time has felt the heavy heel of boss rule. Many of them bear deep scars inflicted by machines of both political persuasions. Yet the hopeful fact is that machine rule has never been able totally to eclipse the public-serving wings of either party and that even big city machines in the classic tradition of corruption are the exception rather than the rule. No machine has proved to be invincible when the public is sufficiently aroused. One after another unsavory political empires have crumbled: the old-style Tammany Hall in New York, the Pendergast Machine in Kansas City, and so forth, have come, conquered—and been ousted. When an organization cannot conceal flagrant misdemeanors a reform tide eventually starts to roll, and sooner or later "the rascals" are turned out. Usually the victor is the opposing party, but occasionally an independent or fusion ticket wins, as was the case with La Guardia in New York and Joseph Clark in Philadelphia.

The danger that any party organization can become ingrown and corrupt is well documented by the history of the one-party system in totalitarian states. If the opposition becomes so weak that it cannot organize a strong protest, it can soon lose the legal right to protest and eventually even to organize. This power-growing capacity of political organizations is not, however, a copyright invention of malevolent dictatorships;

nor even of boss rule. Its potential lies in organization process. Power grows with structure and, in a complex social situation, may attain frightening dimensions. The power of any organization is always a function of its *size, purpose,* and *structure.* The parties in America are leading actors on the political stage, but other huge national organizations play major roles and may upon occasion steal the political show even in the arena of venality.

On the side lines there is always the great formless mass of American citizens; and it has great reserves of strength. Within and without the parties, it continues to hold collectively the power to which even the most entrenched machine can be forced to bow. Though segments of the body politic have succumbed to the blandishments of demagogues and slickly engineered power plays, the whole has never lost its power of resistance, its right to dissent and to organize. This core of strength will not be eroded as long as personal freedom and personal choice remain the beacon lights of private citizenry.

The term "political machine" has come to be applied to a political organization tightly controlled by a small group of insiders. When this happens it is almost inevitable that the resources of the organization will be used to feed the power urge of insiders, if not to line their pockets. To build and maintain their hold, the insiders must be able to fight off all challengers. Thus they are unlikely to be willing to leave organizational control to democratic procedures, although most political machines keep up the fiction, and perhaps some of the forms, of democracy. Behind these fronts, control is held in iron bands.

What is this power which keeps the rank and file toeing the line? The answer is not simple; it is not one power but many. The successful machine controls government jobs, favors, and influence. It is able to reward the faithful with prestige, power, jobs, and money. At the precinct level favors, patronage jobs, even a handout, may be the reward for demonstrated vote-getting ability. Higher up the political scale other assets are coin-of-the-political-realm: bigger favors, more important jobs, an "in" with key persons. Loyalty is an absolute requirement, and machines have scant patience with mavericks and dissidents. If they sometimes appear to tolerate them, it usually is to disarm suspicion, to drain away the will to revolt. Like the nonpolitical elephant, they seldom forget their enemies.

Machines sometimes produce elements of good government; they serve the public when it pays them to do so, and sometimes they can be forced into a show of productive activity. They will go a long way to quiet the clamor of reform, which if allowed to grow would threaten their hold. They make intensive use of the divide-and-conquer routine. They collect garbage at least often enough to prevent an outcry; they put out fires; operate schools; light streets; and so forth. If such services deteriorate to a point where the public's patience is taxed, the machine's applecart may be upset. But characteristically, machine-ridden governments operate far below good performance standards, and at high costs to the public.

A political organization seldom earns the name "machine" unless it is powerful enough to hold the local party in the palm of its hand. Until that degree of control is reached, it is simply a faction or group. But at the point where democratic control ceases, machine organization begins. Thereafter the inner circle is in a position to manipulate organizational rules and procedures, to nominate and elect its own candidates, to control organization coffers and political resources.

It is not easy to build a political machine—or any other kind of political organization, for that matter—and none can long hope to have its power uncontested. The heads that wear the crown are always uneasy because other aspirants for the top positions are never lacking. But there is nothing mysterious about machine organization, for organization is organization whether inside or outside of a machine. The machine hierarchy is layered; there are structural lines and chains of command. Money is raised, personnel recruited, duties assigned, and performance checked. Elections must be won in order to control the coveted instruments of government which give machines their power, and to this end voters are wooed. This is a serious business, and no machine overlooks the strategically important precinct captains. Machines generally oppose civil service procedures because they need jobs for the faithful, and of course they argue that the regulars make the best government officials.

There are similarities but also important differences between the open party organization and the machine. The machine carries personal influence, loyalty, and allegiance to extremes. It metes out rewards and punishments with a stern hand, and it tends to become continuously less squeamish about its methods. If it is well entrenched, it is a good bet that more and more of its activities will slide over into the shadowy land of corruption. Machines need money as well as votes, and the way to get money fast is to send the word down the line that "things are wide open." The machine then moves in to levy heavy tribute on illegal operators whom it protects from the law.

Even when key machine personalities are above taking bribes, they expect each favor to be repaid with interest. They naturally demand that their subordinates deliver the votes and they are often not too particular about the methods that are used to achieve these results. Some of the methods are effective: bought votes and intimidated votes can generally be counted on to turn out at the machine's bidding. A machine-controlled core of votes can provide that nucleus of strength which swings an election. Such blocs of votes are particularly useful in nominating candidates in the primaries, and this is made easier by the fact that many ordinary citizens ignore primaries. In Chicago in 1955 a pattern of controlled votes was unmistakably apparent. Corrupt influences lean heavily on the nonvoting habits of our citizens, an inertia which makes them silent partners of corruption.

Patronage and the Spoils System

Government jobs as well as the ballot box are the objects of every machine's earnest attention.

Political privileges are acquired and used in many ways, and for many purposes, but jobs on the public payrolls are always major plums. The term "payrollers" has come to be applied to organization stalwarts who receive government checks in return for little or no effort expended on the job for which they were ostensibly hired. One house-cleaning raid uncovered one payroller who had illegally received a number of checks totaling thousands of dollars. These were endorsed to and cashed by an alleged relative with a similar name who was also on the public payrolls. The two men turned out to be one and the same person who did not, it might be added, work a double shift for the two sets of checks. Again, it was front-page news when a newly elected city treasurer warned his staff that a full day's work was expected of each employee. He fired one $7000-a-year man for working only one day a week and three other payrollers who were most casual about appearing at the office. Such firings were not cricket in the eyes of the party regulars, and the new treasurer was booed at a large gathering of precinct captains. Offices which have traditionally provided comfortable berths for faithful precinct captains include the county and city clerkships and the departments of building inspection and public works. Bailiffships in the municipal and county courts, particularly in great metropolitan areas, are time-honored sinecures for the faithful.

The process by which political appointees are inserted into public jobs is called the patronage system. Certain key political personages, in and out of government, have acquired rights to fill large numbers of privileged jobs with loyal supporters. Appointees may be personal friends or individuals recommended by accredited—usually party—sponsors. There are well-recognized patronage channels at every level of government. The county central committees (particularly in metropolitan areas) and the state central committees control many patronage jobs, and the patronage rights of United States Senators have been impressive indeed. "Senatorial courtesy," by which major federal appointments in the several states are cleared with the local Senators, is the euphemism which has often cloaked a large-scale patronage operation. Such prerogatives remain substantial even though many coveted federal plums are now blanketed under civil service. Until the postal service was recently put under civil service it was the patronage prize par excellence. Tens of thousands of postmasterships across the country were regularly used to pay off campaign debts, a practice which made the Postmaster General a key political figure.

Although the merit system is slowly drying up the stream of political jobs, patronage remains a powerful political weapon. In 1953 the Republicans, job-starved after twenty years in exile from Washington, naturally went over federal jobs with a fine-tooth comb looking for spots for deserving Republicans, and the Republican National Committee clearance procedures took on new importance. This is standard political practice and such earnest reshuffling goes on whenever one party is ousted and the other takes over. Sweeping party victories always pound away against the civil service floor that is built under government jobs. But in spite of this fact the merit system is steadily being reinforced and its pilings are being more deeply sunk (of the 430 employees in the U.S. Bureau of the Budget in 1957, only 5 were exempted from the regular civil service).

Jobs are only one part of the spoils system; there are other government assets which play important roles in consolidating the hold of a political organization. Where there is outright corruption administrative, legislative, even judicial, favors are bought and sold. Public work contracts have proven to be a fertile field for such activities. If unusually lucrative arrangements are too bald-faced a fraud on the public, there are other ways of seeing that a low bid can still be made to produce high profits. Substandard materials may be substituted, inspections may be superficial or conveniently blind, and corners can be cut behind sympathetic official backs. The sums involved are sometimes large, and a strong temptation to both sides in the extralegal exchange. Muckrakers at the beginning of the century, in the footsteps of Lincoln Steffins, uncovered frauds so appalling as to rouse even an apathetic public. Some of the more lurid tales centered around huge profits made at the expense of public institutions. Incredible conditions in penal and other state institutions have been found to be closely tied to illegal profits for those who supplied food and other services and commodities. The same supplies had even been sold *twice* to the same public institution.

The sale of public licenses and franchises can also be lucrative. In the last half-century government regulatory commissions have come to exercise life or death power over certain areas of private business. Small wonder that affected interests have occasionally exerted pressures on legislatures and administrators in the hopes of modifying such regulatory activities. The muckrakers had rich soil for their tilling in such pressures and uncovered many cynical alliances between businesses and government officials where key party figures undertook the lucrative role of middleman. The notorious trusts of the 1890s played their part in this story, and some of the pressure for trust-busting came from the disclosure that concentrated economic power was corrupting the processes of democratic government. The era of the great industrial octopi coincided with the emergence of powerful machine bosses and the two sometimes became cynically intertwined. The rewards of such unholy alliances were gold-plated and diamond-studded, and political bosses were often able to put legislators as well as administrators on the leash.

Picturesque, if horrifying, accounts of political deals speckle our political history. The "notorious Artie Samish, lobby potentate of California," has fascinated every observer. The United States Senate Special Crime Committee (1951) described his activities thus:

The strange tale of the part played by an almost unbelievable character, Arthur H. Samish, in the California picture nearly defies description. Mr. Samish can safely be called "Mr. Big" in California. His physical weight, around 300 pounds, can be calculated fairly accurately but the weight of his influence in the affairs of that State would be most difficult to estimate. Mr. Samish describes himself as a "public relations counsel" or a "policy consultant" and has declared on at least one occasion, "I am the legislature." [2]

Samish was reported to represent the Association of State Brewers who, over a period of six years, put some $500,000 at his disposal. When one Senator asked:

". . . When it comes up as to whether a proposed referendum is to be good or bad for the brewing industry, whether an election of a State Senator, a member of the legislature or the passage of a bill in the legislature will be good or bad, that decision is made exclusively and wholly by Mr. Samish?" The answer of the Secretary of the California State Brewers Institute was, "That is my understanding: Yes." [3]

Liquor interests and manufacturers of slot machines and other gambling devices are under continuous pressure from the underworld elements. Racketeers live by levying tribute, and their stock in trade is lucrative tie-ups with local authorities which enable them to provide protection for "wide-open

[2] Third Interim Report of the Special Committee to investigate Organized Crime in Interstate Commerce, Senate Report No. 307, 82nd Congress, First Session (Washington: U.S. Govt. Printing Office, 1951), p. 100.
[3] *Ibid.*, p. 101.

operations." But unhappily other businesses have not always been above using political pressures to achieve profitable ends. Otherwise legitimate businesses have bought their share of legislators, bribed administrators, intimidated competitors, corrupted the police, and blindfolded justice.

Who is corrupting whom?

Which leads to an important question: Who is corrupting whom? Someone pays for the favors that are bought; someone hands out the bribes. Some private interest stands to profit; and someone shuts his eyes to what his conscience would rather not see. The unhappy fact is that much political corruption must be placed on the doorstep of legitimate business and supposedly upright citizens. The syndicate and the venal police officer are not the only villains in the piece. Their teamplay is made possible by public complacency. The Senate Crime Committee and other investigators have made it clear that there can be no continuing tie-up between crime and politics without the silent nod of key public officials. Such men are answerable to the public, yet the public has failed to enforce the law. For all the cries of "dirty politics" and "racketeers," the fact is that public apathy and public ignorance must bear their full share of responsibility.

The everyday citizen must also accept his share of responsibility for this case of public schizophrenia. All too often he is anxious to fix a traffic ticket or is willing to wink at or sidestep one law or another. Robbers, burglars, purse-snatchers frequently escape prosecution because their victims refuse to go to the trouble of preferring charges. The landlord who shabbily, even dangerously, converts his property so that it becomes a profitable slum; the black marketeer; the tax evader—all these and many others are tarred with the same brush. Yet they may all be churchgoers, good neighbors with reputations for being solid citizens, and none of them may have ever short-penciled a ballot or sold his vote.

None of us is free from the temptation to get around some inconvenient law. But when it is suggested that you "make a little present to an alderman to put a NO PARKING, COUNCIL ORDER sign in front of your house," it might be well to remember that little bribes can swell to mighty oceans of corruption. Many observers have pointed out that Americans like to see what they can get by with. We congratulate ourselves on getting something for nothing, perhaps something we do not deserve. A little soul-searching is indicated to see if such private personal practices can be reconciled with our public indignation at corruption and dirty politics.

We are outraged when a tie-up between crime and politics breaks into open scandal, but how many of us are even momentarily concerned to see that the police and other government officials are paid enough so that they can afford the luxury of being honest? Honest politics demands more than honest citizens; it demands knowledgeable and participating citizens. It also demands high (and enforced) standards of public service, and the citizen-politician must insist on such service.

The Importance of the Political Professional

Professionalism in politics has two facets: the legitimate and the illegitimate. Because the stakes are high and the risk great, illegitimate politics organizes to the hilt. Such organization has important lessons for the citizen-politician, for it silhouettes the basic processes of political organization and puts citizens on notice concerning the shady tricks of the political trade. Thus there is much more to an excursion behind corruption than sensationalism. It is part of the process of charting the reaches of political activity. A quick plunge into its murky depths is part of the toughening process which every would-be citizen-politician needs. If you are to be truly effective in what is often a deadly serious political fight, you cannot afford the luxury of a sweetness-and-light approach.

However, professionalism in politics is not all sensational and tawdry. Professionalism is at work on the side of the citizen as well as against him. There is a growing superstructure of institutions and practices which is providing sturdy foundations for democratic government. We have pointed to increasingly hopeful developments in the art of practical politics, in public administration, and in professionalism in the best and most democratic sense. But civic-minded professionalism inside the political parties remains uniquely the responsibility of the citizen-politician.

The American political scene is full of paradoxes; but perhaps one of the strangest is the suspicion and contempt which in many circles has come to color the term "professional politician." This disrespect has occasionally been fully earned, but this country has also produced many selfless and dedicated political servants who have done their day-to-day tasks in party and public service and have helped to forward the growth of the democratic ideal. This has taken grinding work and great vision. Our public services and the two great parties have had to keep government processes growing right along with the challenges that characterize our atomic age. This takes professionalism of a high order.

By and large our public servants are devoted, able—and underpaid. To say that in the oversized barrel of 7 million government employees there is room for many rotten apples is not to condone laziness, greed, corruption, or subversion. Rather it is to face the fact that human nature and human institutions cannot be expected to bring to the acme of perfection so many millions of public servants. Government employees are a typical cross-section of Americans, displaying a reasonable sample of their virtues and a full measure of loyalty to American institutions. Despite the fact that scores of thousands of these public servants have firsthand encounters with partisanship, favoritism, subversion, even corruption, they retain a solid core of respect for the public service. They understand as few outsiders can the problems, the headaches, the compromises, and the muddling through which democratic government demands of its servants. And the number of non-voters in this group is much fewer than in the public at large.

From the national level on down, there are hopeful signs of growing respect for government service and political action— in spite of occasional scandals or loyalty investigations run wild. But where public service and the political parties attain real prestige they reflect the stature of statesmenlike Presidents, Senators, cabinet heads, governors, mayors, and other good public servants. The contribution and dedication of distinguished citizens who serve with little financial reward and often in the face of slanderous public attack are helping to erode prejudice against the public service.

But the best antidote for the down-the-nose view of politics is more active participation by citizen-politicians. This is the surest road to broadened understanding of government, of political parties, and of the relationship of the citizen to his government. Such participation is in fact the challenge of our times, the final test of whether or not democratic processes can be kept truly responsive to the wishes of the people.

PART III

Political Action: The Art of the Possible

CHAPTER SEVEN

Political Action: The Art of the Possible

CITIZEN ATTITUDES AND CITIZEN PARTICIPATION

The crux of citizen participation in government lies deep inside each of us and it centers in our attitudes toward politics. Since attitudes are the mainsprings of human motivation they determine whether we make the real effort that participation in politics requires. One of the most serious aspects of widespread apathy and cynicism is the effect it has on neighbors and friends but most importantly on our children. Civic inaction spreads cancerlike into civic deterioration.

The contagion of cynicism

A high school civics teacher once invited one of the authors to speak to her class. When he demurred because of the press of time and the remoteness of the school, she responded, "But, Alderman, there isn't a single youngster in this whole class who believes there is such a thing as an honest politician. I want them to see one." Naturally the alderman met the class. He discovered that the teacher had not exaggerated and he tried to find out the reasons for such negative attitudes. One boy reported that he had worked a whole summer in a handbook (illegal horse-betting parlor) and had seen police officers regularly coming in and some of them getting paid off for protection. Another had a friend who got into some scrape and bought his way out. A third had heard his father and another man talking about fixing a traffic ticket. These were boys from an average middle-class neighborhood. With such experiences how could their attitudes toward government be uncorroded?

The whole question of civic attitudes is a major challenge to democracy, a challenge more serious in many ways than the external threat of communism. Undermined confidence in ourselves, in our way of life, is the most insidious of all threats. To prevent such paralysis is a first responsibility of citizen-politicians. The vicious cycle of inertia and corruption must be cut through somewhere. Our public servants are on the first line of defense. If we insist that they shall become shining examples of rectitude we must also change the cynical attitudes of citizens, and help to undercut the common civic disease of moral laziness.

Civic virtue and civic vice are habit-forming. Take the cases of Phenix City, Alabama, and Columbus, Georgia, across the river from one another. Phenix City became so embedded in corruption that its political bosses did not even stop at murder; it took the National Guard to clean up the town in the early 1950s. But Columbus had no such history. The people in those two communities are not poured from different molds yet they tolerated very different sorts of public behavior. As one businesswoman in Phenix City put it:

We just took our government for granted too long, and when people do that, things like the Phenix City situation result. Every so often in history, a generation comes along which is not too interested in its government. They realize too late that you can't take your government for granted and expect it to run smoothly for the benefit of everybody. Gangsters didn't take our government for granted. They just took it.

Cities have been most susceptible to organized corruption,

although not all cities have fallen victim to this civic disease and certainly not all officials in those cities which have felt the "bite" are complacent, cooperative with the wrong elements, or corrupt. But the Senate Crime Committee's revelations in 1949 and 1950, and the 1957 Senate probe of suspected labor-racketeering, shocked the whole nation into an awareness of the extent to which organized criminal elements had dug themselves into the political and government life of many cities. Some of the stories which came to the attention of the Chicago City Council's crime committee are among the most sordid tales of municipal corruption. Even respectable citizens came to expect that most officials make a little money on the side. A large gasoline company official told one of the committee, "It is nice to know that if we put up a filling station in your ward, we won't have to pay anything for a driveway permit" (to which he had a legal right).

One should not conclude from such tales that there is no hope for better government. One area after another has cleaned itself up, and in general the level of public integrity ascends as we go up the government ladder. But it is grave disservice to every one of the millions of honest public employees to tolerate those who are giving public service, politics, and democratic government a black eye. And the resulting corrosion of civic attitudes is even more costly.

Civic attitudes and voting behavior: report on a study of the 1955 Chicago mayoral election [1]

Citizen attitudes and citizen habits are closely tied together. And both increasingly are being subjected to close scrutiny by political scientists and pollsters. Significant studies have been made,[2] but we are still a long way from being able to

[1] This section was prepared with the assistance of Leo Shapiro, now of Leo Shapiro Associates, and Robert Stierer and George Rosenbaum.

[2] H. F. Gosnell, *Negro Politicians* (Chicago: University of Chicago Press, 1933); C. E. Merriam and H. Gosnell, *Nonvoting* (Chicago: Uni-

prescribe a treatment which will overcome widespread lack of citizen participation. To learn more of what makes voters and nonvoters the University of Chicago, utilizing foundation funds, sponsored a survey of the Chicago 1955 mayoralty election. This survey was conducted for the university by Science Research Associates. They used the same probability sampling technique that was used by the Merriam organization during the campaign itself. The study was prompted by the fact that some 600,000 registered Chicago voters (more than 30 per cent of all registered voters) did not vote in that election. The study unearthed a storehouse of information and only the highlights can be given here.[3]

Voting, like most human actions, is influenced by the habits instilled in young citizens in their formative years. Regular voting patterns are found in families in which there has been a continuing interest in politics. Those who participate most actively and vote most consistently (and they total about 25 per cent of the population twenty-one years old and over) have early memories of family interest in politics. They frequently report remembering that their parents voted regularly and talked politics at home. The excitement of campaigning and speechmaking impressed them; they even remembered issues and the candidates whom their parents supported in a particular election, and who won. They felt proud and important the first time they voted, although they were scared or nervous. In the Chicago mayoral election almost four out of five persons in this category went to the polls.

There is a second group, at the other end of the political

---

versity of Chicago Press, 1924); B. R. Berelson, P. F. Lazarsfeld and W. N. McPhee, *Voting* (Chicago: University of Chicago Press, 1954); Sam Lubell, *The Future of American Politics* (New York: Harper & Brothers, 1952).

[3] Report on *A Survey of Some Aspects of Voting and Nonvoting in The Chicago 1955 Mayoral Election*, conducted by Science Research Associates for the University of Chicago (released by the University of Chicago, November 1955).

spectrum, who never vote. They made up about 10 per cent of the population of voting age. This group had never established the voting habit although they may occasionally have shown some mild interest in a particular election. Typically, they say their reason for not voting is "lack of interest," "ignorance of politics," "lack of time," or "just not having gotten around to registering."

The remaining two-thirds of potential voters were likely to have fluctuating voting records. The unstable voting patterns of this group are reflected in the large differences in turnout from one election to the next. They generally voted at least once, but their political behavior fell into one of three general categories (although there were minor shifts from election to election): (1) There are those who were somewhat interested but did not get around to voting; (2) there are others who voted but showed no further interest; and (3) there are those who voted and expressed interest but who did not participate in any campaign activities. About 60 per cent of the people in this group voted in the Chicago mayoral election. Members of this group seem to have felt their duty was fulfilled by casting a vote, though occasionally they offered excuses for not being able to do more. None of them reported campaigning or otherwise participating in politics in any election.

There is encouraging evidence however that once a person has advanced up the scale in civic participation he rarely backslides, even a notch. Once a direct participant in politics, he tends to remain active. As a person grows older and gains more experience in more elections the likelihood of his voting increases. The Chicago survey bears this out. On the average there was a fourteen-year age difference between the active participant, who was forty-seven, and the disinterested non-voter, who was thirty-three. Three-fourths of the persons in the fifty to sixty-four year group voted in the mayoral election, while slightly less than half of the persons in the twenty-one to thirty-four year group went to the polls. This suggests that active citizen participation in any given election can have long-range cumulative results by adding to the number of consistent voters at each subsequent election.

Those who never vote were generally reluctant or unable to explore their reasons. Few of them were willing to say that they were against voting in general, or even that everyone involved in politics is crooked. A handful did answer this way. More generally some feeble excuse was given. Happily, this study showed that most of the interviewees thought everyone should vote, and those who did not vote usually just had not formed the habit. The survey further indicated that the apathetic group had no strong reasons for not voting; they had simply failed to develop the habit, often because they had not established roots in the community. Only one out of ten of these nonvoters was a home owner and more than half of them had lived at their address for no more than one year. Negroes, who generally do not share equally in opportunities for establishing communal ties, were heavily represented in this group.

But voting is not the only aspect of citizen participation in elections, much less in government. The survey also threw light on the other forms of civic participation. In the campaign in which interviewees reported they had worked hardest, the following types of activity were predominant:

   7% canvassed.
   9% did other volunteer work.
   5% contributed money.
   19% went to one or more meetings.
   13% met or saw a candidate in person.
   41% tried to influence their friends.[4]

The potential effectiveness of precinct work in turning out the vote was also indicated by this study. Queried concerning

[4] These figures cannot be totaled, for some persons reported more than one kind of activity.

visits by a precinct captain during the campaign, nearly twice as many voters as nonvoters reported such a visit.

When questioned as to why the election in which they worked hardest was most important to them, they reported the following reasons:

33% supported one of the candidates.
 5% were opposed to one candidate.
17% found specific issues particularly significant.
14% were affected personally by the election.
10% had party considerations.
 5% had other reasons.
16% did not answer.

Thus faith in a candidate was the largest single factor in explaining the high point of political participation in the lives of these respondents. The survey further reflected this faith in the fact that seven out of eight respondents thought their man would win.

What conclusions can be drawn from these facts?

1. Perhaps most important: voting habits are tremendously important. Generally they are formed early. Family history and childhood election experience appear to be key factors. Once acquired, interest tends to be sustained and more active participation becomes likely.

2. Active political work in any given election is limited to a relatively small proportion of the public, but as people become involved in such activity they almost always vote and are active in later elections.

3. Political coming-of-age for most people does not coincide with attaining voting age; it comes after recurrent experience with elections. In broadening citizen participation it is perhaps more important to lower the average age of active political participation from fifty to twenty-one than to lower the legal voting age from twenty-one to eighteen, although we favor the latter as well.

Mr. Leo Shapiro summarized his findings thus:

The desire to vote is not something which is inherited or something which is innate in the soul of every citizen. When there is a failure to vote, it is not because citizens instinctively desire to vote but are frustrated by bad weather, or a revulsion to corruption in politics, by illness, or by some other diversionary force. Rather, the nonvoter typically is apathetic, disinterested, and not inclined to vote unless something happens to make him want to vote.

The desire to vote, the inclination to vote, is something that is acquired over a period of time and from a variety of sources. The family in which a child is raised is crucial. Has he had an opportunity to observe his parents voting, has he seen them show real interest in politics, and do something active about it? If this sort of experience is in his background there is a better chance that he will take an active part in public affairs or will at least cast his vote. This does not mean that the effect of schools, newspapers, and public information media should be underestimated. . . .

This survey indicates that childhood family experience, early voting experience, quality of candidates, and campaigns all have cumulative effects. Thus the struggle to get out the vote is not won or lost in the few weeks that precede a specific election. It is something which must be worked for and earned by all of us at the family dinner table, in the schoolroom, and in political party gatherings. Each campaign in which there are good candidates, important issues, and vigorous public debate, adds to the all too small number of citizens who will take an active role in public affairs. To increase their numbers our research indicates that campaigns should be carried back to the home where children get an opportunity to see their parents and other important grown-ups actively involved and where such participation is accepted as important.

In any one election, the voters who participate most actively are probably less than 5 per cent of the total. But such voters are voters for life although they may not do precinct work, contribute money, or otherwise participate actively in successive elections. By the age of 50 most citizens have been faced with the kind of public issues which contribute to the development of consistent voters. In one sense the success of a campaign depends on whether or not citizens by the time they are 21 have received the kind of political experience that would make them fairly consistent voters. We need to increase the political life expectancy of our citizens by helping them come of age politically before they are 50 years old.

It is an interesting if paradoxical fact that American citizens, even if they do not vote or participate in political campaigns, like to consider themselves as voters and participants, and of course they want to be identified with the winner. Since everybody thinks of himself as a voter, most nonvoters will not readily listen to exhortations to vote because they will say to themselves, "They're talking about some other guy." Appeals to get out the vote might be more effective if they were addressed to "You citizens who vote consistently, be sure to vote in this election," rather than "You non-voters, get out and vote!"

From time to time people have urged compulsory voting laws as an answer to citizen apathy. Some countries, notably Belgium, Switzerland, and Australia, have tried various forms of compulsion with some success. But a number of difficulties stand in the way of any such plan for America. To begin with it would require coordinated state legislative action across the nation. And there would be judicial barriers to overcome; Kansas City tried obligatory voting and it was declared unconstitutional by the Missouri Supreme Court. But the major obstacle lies in the fact that the whole idea of such compulsion runs counter to American traditions. Voters in Oregon rejected it in 1920, and although the constitutions of Massachusetts and North Dakota both allow it, neither state has taken action.

Forcing people to vote is not the answer, but as we have pointed out much could be accomplished through improved election procedures as well as by broadening civic education. The multiplicity of elections which face every voter has contributed to public confusion and apathy, and ballots of gargantuan proportions are no encouragement to timid or indolent citizens.

THE POWER OF ONE

Voting is important but it is only the first and most elementary step of participation by citizen-politicians. It is the most obvious and most exciting part, in many ways, but the accumulation of the force of one plus one plus one can be felt in other ways as well. This accumulation of citizen power, both inside and outside the parties, is the touchstone of effective citizenship. To most people a single vote sounds like a puny weapon for tackling the problems of our times. Yet however great one's personal humility, it remains true that the sum total of many small strengths can be a powerful makeweight in our political scheme of things. When one plus one plus one . . . unite their feeble strengths, the scales of government and the scales of party power tip. This is the central fact of political democracy and the parties themselves operate on its terms, because it works.

Proof of the pudding

No precinct committeeman overlooks the power of one, and none writes off an opposition even though it can be counted on the fingers of one hand. The smaller the precinct the more important each vote. If a precinct of two hundred registered voters has its usual proportion of nonvoters, the effective votes may be cut down to one hundred; 51 per cent of these (or about a quarter of the total registered vote) will then carry that precinct. If Democrats and Republicans are almost evenly divided, a mere baker's dozen of uncommitted votes will tip the election scales. This is why a small group of determined voters can often swing an election.

But even in less advantageous situations the power of one is greater than most people assume. It is sharply magnified in any close contest; and since political decisions are always full of uncertainties, no one can be presumed to be expendable.

Literally hundreds of examples showing the power of one

can be found in the pages of political history. Perhaps the most dramatic was in the presidential election of 1876. Rutherford B. Hayes was declared the victor over Samuel Tilden by an electoral college vote of 185 to 184. Because so many state election returns were disputed, a special commission was appointed by the Congress to certify the winning electors from the disputed states. The special commission voted eight to seven to accept the Hayes electors. And in one state one of the Hayes electors had won by one vote. One of the people who voted for the winning elector was an old man so sick he had to be carried to the polling place on a stretcher. But he insisted on going. Did that one old man elect President Hayes? Of course not, but if he had not voted the result would have been different.

President Grover Cleveland defeated James G. Blaine in the 1884 election by 219 to 182 electoral votes. The New York vote went to Cleveland by 1149 votes out of 1,125,159 cast. Less than one vote per precinct would have given New York, and the election, to Blaine. President Woodrow Wilson defeated Charles Evans Hughes in 1916 by 277 to 254 electoral votes. The California electoral vote went to Wilson by a margin of 3806 votes out of nearly 1 million cast. Less than one vote per precinct more for Hughes in each of the 5000 precincts in the state would have given the state and the election to Hughes. In fact Hughes went to bed on election night believing that he had won California and the election. In 1948 President Harry Truman defeated Thomas E. Dewey in one of the real upsets of modern presidential voting. Dewey lost Ohio by 7107 votes, and California by 17,865 votes, each a margin of about one vote per precinct. A different result in these two states would have thrown the election into the House of Representatives.

In 1954 Governor Averell Harriman of New York was elected by a margin of 11,125 votes out of 5,110,351 cast in 10,437 precincts; Governor Milward Simpson of Wyoming was elected by 1112 votes; and Senator Clifford Case of New Jersey was elected by 3370 votes out of 1,719,686 cast in 3992 precincts, to mention some of the tightly contested races of that year.

In 1956 more than the usual number of close contests were recorded. We already have mentioned the Rhode Island gubernatorial race (Chapter Five). All through the long night of November 6 and well into the next day (and sometimes for many days), weary election workers counted and recounted the ballots in dozens of tight contests. The political fate of key Representatives, Senators, and governors hung in many a precarious balance. Representative Hale of Maine was reelected by 29 votes; Senator Case of South Dakota was first declared the loser, then certified as winner— his margin was 4620 votes; Congressman Holmes of Washington won by 1250 votes; Representative Chenoweth of Colorado won by 695 votes; Congressman Sieminski of New Jersey was also declared the loser, then certified as victor by 57 votes (first reports had him losing by one vote, then winning by two votes); Representative Doliver of Iowa lost by 198 votes; and Representative Delaney of New York won by 102 votes. Talk to any one of these men, or their opponents, if you still do not think *your* vote may be needed.

The power of one is registered elsewhere than at the voting booth. Individual leaders can accomplish much and they need not be dyed-in-the-wool politicians to make their weight felt.

In 1923 a young Cincinnati lawyer began a movement for a new city government that broke the power of the machine that controlled the banks and much of the business of the city as well as the judges and the police force.

The political machine begun in Louisiana by Huey Long and continued by his brother was defeated after many years, chiefly through the efforts of a single person, Judge Robert Kennon, who was elected Governor on the basis of his program.

An Oregon woman, disgusted with the vice, gambling, and corruption in her city, worked in her precinct and developed such a large following that eventually she was elected Mayor of Portland and succeeded in putting across her "clean city" program (at least temporarily).

A graduate law student at Harvard once sparked the whole city of Boston in reorganizing the government and deposing Boss Curley.

And the drawings of a political cartoonist, Thomas Nast, were largely responsible for breaking up the notorious Tammany-Boss Tweed rule in New York City.[5]

More recently, the clean-up of Phenix City was spearheaded by outraged citizens.

Every reform measure starts in the head of one person. When such a person wins the support of enough others he can sometimes accomplish miracles. There are all sorts of ways of amplifying a single voice but the surest way is to blend it with that of other like-minded individuals. The successes of the special interest lobbies are a case in point. Mr. Truman early in 1955 pointed out that some 15 million persons are strongly represented in Washington by professional lobbyists. Such men have know-how and connections, but their ultimate source of power is the bloc of votes they represent. When a lobbyist's voice is further upheld by that of distinguished citizen leaders it becomes powerfully persuasive.

Private ways of exerting political pressures

But all the power in the world means little unless applied strategically. The locating of strategic targets was considered earlier; here the emphasis is on ways of focusing citizen pressures. The channels are many; sometimes one or another is to be preferred, but frequently several devices are used to reinforce each other. *Petitions* with impressive numbers of signatures are a favored device. These can be helpfully reinforced by *personal letters*, but it is difficult to inspire letters in im-

[5] R. E. Merriam and J. W. Bethea, *Understanding Politics* (Chicago: Science Research Associates pamphlets, 1952).

pressive numbers. Every letter-writing campaign has many
hurdles to take. First there is the matter of the salutation or
mode of address. Should it be addressed to "The Honorable,"
"The Right Honorable," "Senator," and so forth? Such "emily-
postisms" tend to raise barriers that inhibit timid or lukewarm
correspondents. Then there is the form of the message. Will a
postcard do, or should it be a letter? Should it be personally
written? Is it enough to go on record for or against, or should
one spell out one's position in some detail? Is it true that a
nose count is all that interests the recipient? Does he literally
weigh the flood of messages that come to him?

The weight of numbers is always important, but masses of
identical messages are a dead giveaway that the letter campaign was inspired by some interested group; it lacks the sense
of spontaneous pressure which thoughtful individual messages
convey. The organizer of a letter campaign will be well
advised to prepare instructions which include:

1. The full name, address, and recommended salutation of
addressee.

2. A brief statement of the issue and the recommended
position, perhaps supplemented by one or more model letters.

3. An injunction to put the message in the correspondent's
own words, but to use the "canned" message rather than to
put off writing.

4. A target date and the reasons for its selection.

5. A request for a report back where practicable (including
a summary of the message and the answer received).

Such campaigns need to be carefully timed to allow for the
build-up of the flow of letters to the target office at a time
when it will produce the best results. This should not be left
to chance. The success of many a campaign has reflected the
artful application of waves of pressure as action moved along.
Thus letters to the Congress may usefully take the following
pattern: First letters to one's own Congressman urging the
introduction (or action upon) a bill near to one's heart; then

letters to key figures on the committees of the House or Senate to which it is referred; possibly second letters to urge the reporting out of the measure if it appears to have become strategically lost or buried in committee; more letters then to one's representative urging support when the bill appears on the floor; still more letters when the bill goes to the other house where a repetition of similar pressures may also be called for; still more letters to the conference committee that will iron out differences between the House and Senate measures; and finally letters to the President to urge him to sign or veto the completed measure.

While legislators are a natural target for aroused citizen reaction, administrators too may need to be reminded of the public's wishes. Even the President gets thousands of letters weekly from all sorts of people on all sorts of subjects, and these numbers skyrocket when an issue becomes intense. All of these letters are carefully read by someone in the White House and most are referred to the agencies concerned. One Senator from a populous state reports that his mail averages several thousand letters a week.

There are other pressures that, if somewhat less direct, are also helpful in persuading politicians and public servants; these involve the use of publicity techniques. The familiar "letters to the editor" is useful in keeping public opinion focused and boiling. Publicizing the views of experts or well-known persons, releases to the membership of key organizations, public distribution of flyers, pamphlets, and other literature all will help to crystallize, motivate, and focus citizen pressure. The systematic organization of group pressures through the familiar device of the joint committee is also a tested—and demanding—procedure.

Such pressures can be intensified by attendance at open hearings of public bodies. City councils, boards of education, and the courts usually have open meetings. If the public takes the trouble to attend, its presence strongly reinforces those who are working in the public's interest. But if private citizens do not bother to show up, it is scarcely surprising that the public or party officials tend to minimize the strength of the public's concern.

It is important to stress the fact that effective citizen pressure depends on speaking the *right words into the right ears.* The shortest distance to key persons is as important as accurate and astute timing. Upholding the right hand at just the right minute can deal the lethal blow to one's opponents.

There are facets of citizen pressure that deserve a word of caution. There is always danger that individuals—and groups —will go off half-cocked. Wanton words can do much damage and waste valuable energy. Naïve, careless people often seriously harm a good cause, and they are open to being used by a bad one. To avoid prostituting one's citizen powers each individual owes himself a debt of caution and investigation. This is easier said than done. The world's problems are so complicated, the threads of interest so interwoven and some-times camouflaged that it is difficult to untangle twisted strands of pressures, much less align them on the beam of the public interest. Yet this is a grave and basic responsibility of citizens in a democracy. Wise and effective civic effort requires politi-cal skill that must be learned and cultivated. Fortunately such skills can grow from the roots of systematic individual partici-pation.

To the cynic who will say or think that letters or personal visits have no effect on the hard-bitten politician, we can only respond "It isn't so." Your authors, both as letter-writers and recipients, can tell you that your representatives, both elected and appointed, *do* read their mail, they *do* pay attention to what is said, they *do* consider such views, and often they are influenced by such representations. And this applies even to the most entrenched machine politician. It is easy to rational-ize laziness or inaction by saying that it does not matter what one individual thinks. But how can any individual in a democ-racy, where he is all-important, really believe this?

Service as a citizen-politician is fully as important to our country's future as service as a citizen-soldier, and a great deal less dangerous. When the chips are down in wartime, democracy's secret weapon has always been the dedication of its citizen-soldiers. Dictators and their like never have understood this strength of democracy. They choose to think we are soft and decadent (indeed we are sometimes slow starters, but we always manage to prove our mettle). The hope for a democratic future depends on our ability to transfer this spirit of participation and cooperation to our civic concerns. Strong armies of citizen-politicians are vital in our march toward unlimited horizons. These armies can work most directly and generally most efficiently through the parties of their choice, but when such channels appear blocked there are detours inside and outside of party action which the citizen-politician can take to arrive at his civic goals.

THE ART OF THE POSSIBLE

Progress by inches is often the best one can hope for in politics. If one combs history it is possible to uncover instances where breathtaking changes were quickly accomplished, but by and large an inching progress is the pattern; indeed one must often be delighted with any signs of progress at all. Reformers are wont to overlook this fact and often give up in the darkness that precedes the dawn. Most of the government reforms we have mentioned have required long, patient build-ups.

The fact that most political change creeps forward at something less than a snail's pace often causes citizens to become impatient, then discouraged, and finally resigned to their presumed political fate. The professional politician is more of a realist; he has come to terms with the glacial pace of political change. For example, when a flurry of reform opposition raises a storm, an experienced machine boss furls his sails, battens down the hatches, and prepares to ride out the storm.

He counts on the fact that most citizen protests are short-lived. When the storm passes he unfurls his sails, opens the hatches, and resumes his course. One of the hardest things for the citizen-politician to accept is the fact that political achievements are the reward of a long-distance race, not a quick sprint.

Planning the political attack

Astute political maneuvers depend on accurate diagnoses which, if superficial, can easily miss the target. Case histories of the aches and pains that afflict the body politic must be examined carefully; symptoms must be traced back to remote as well as proximate causes. The prescribed cure must take in all contributing factors. For example, it is not sufficient to establish an enlightened housing code if inspection is lax or inspectors are corrupt. Administrative procedures and the capacities and integrity of administrators are often as important as the ordinances or laws themselves. And any forward push must be strongly backed by an alert citizenry. Political diagnoses, whether exercised by reformers or machine bosses, require the experienced feeling of many kinds of pulses.

After the diagnosis is complete the campaign must be carefully planned and executed. This process involves jockeying for position, lining up support, and steering along a sometimes difficult course. Often the path is heavily overhung with the fog of conflicting interests. All politicians must pick their allies with care, judging their strength, their loyalty, and their usefulness in the struggle at hand. Often they must take what they can get and make the best of it. Eager neophytes may find to their chagrin that they are being used for purposes far from their intent. The citizen-politician is urged to learn how to pick his allies, to pick them with care, and to be sure that they are not picking him. The practiced politician finds his way through all such perplexities to create almost miraculously a whole that is greater than the sum of the parts.

One of the most difficult tasks of politics is also one of the most important: the art of timing. Experienced politicians come to react almost automatically in many situations, but most decisions profit by careful thought and planning. Astute timing involves such problems as these: What issues should be brought up, and when? How should they be stated or presented? Is this the time to fight or should one beat a strategic retreat and wait for more auspicious circumstances? Such questions are faced by every officeholder, civic group, political party, or private citizen interested in politics or government.

How does the individual legislator or the citizen lobbyist decide what issues to promote when there are hundreds of matters before him? The following prescriptions may be helpful:

1. *Know your issue.* Never enter a debate unless you know what you are talking about. Does this sound too elementary? Read any legislative journal, even the *Congressional Record,* and you will be amazed to see how often this elementary precaution is ignored. This rule also applies to appearances before legislative or administrative committees. How one cringes for the individual pleading a good cause who is led to slaughter when his lack of preparation is laid bare! Of all the weaknesses demonstrated by civic organizations in their dealings with government bodies, inadequate preparation and presentation lead the rest.

2. *Establish priorities.* Whether legislator, administrator, or citizen, one must exercise selectivity. Too many balls in the air at the same time diffuse interest and attention and important matters may get lost. Pick the issues most important to *you* and fight for them one at a time.

3. *Plan your attack.* Every public issue, no matter what its virtues, needs to have its way prepared. *This is important.* If, for example, the issue is a higher minimum hourly wage, get national columnists, economists, professional groups, legisla-

tors, administrators, and citizen organizations thinking about the matter before you move.

4. *Stick to the essentials.* Organize your case so that it can be understood by the lowest common denominator of your potential support. Be clear and precise; leave out interesting but extraneous sidelights. Many a good idea has gone down the drain when its proponents fell into the trap of becoming involved in lengthy arguments about inconsequential details.

5. *Dramatize your issue.* Do not be a sensationalist, but remember that what you have to say must compete with many other interests, some of which may be dramatic. So be factual but interesting. Solid showmanship is important.

6. *Be persistent.* Many a promising campaign has foundered because its supporters gave up when success was almost in sight. Remember that everything takes time, especially in politics, and cultivate the necessary patience to put over your program. The economy bloc in the Chicago City Council pounded away year after year at certain vulnerable spots in the city budget until they finally forced action. It was a long pull; 101 amendments involving $6 million were proposed, but only one item for $13 was passed in the first year. Three years later, however, more than one-half of the savings originally proposed were in effect. And since then still others have been acted upon. The seeds of good ideas are tough and germinal.

It is sometimes hard to content oneself with inaction when all around there is so much that needs doing. And yet the quickest way to failure—and political oblivion—is to barge ahead without a proper respect for the delicate requirements of good timing. One of the authors, when he was alderman, proposed a plan to use women as school-crossing guards in order to release seven hundred policemen for necessary service elsewhere. Women can do this work as well or better than policemen, they cost one-third as much, and they free the policemen for full-time crime fighting or crime prevention.

The idea was not original at the time; it had worked out advantageously before then in many places. It had even been suggested earlier to the City Council, but the original sponsor had not followed it through.

There were all sorts of problems in promoting this proposal, for neither the mayor, the police commissioner, nor the majority in the City Council was originally behind it. The first move was to collect information on how the plan had worked in other places, how much they paid the women, and so forth. The next move was to get policemen to testify that crossing duty left them little time for other more serious duties. Then followed a series of meetings with PTA's and other interested civic organizations. Delegations went to see their aldermen, to soften them up. Regional safety councils, composed of people from business, school, and civic groups, were enlisted. Talks were made all over the city. The newspapers were visited one by one; editorials and articles emphasizing the common-sense nature of this proposal were obtained. The plan took on the name of the Merriam School Guard Plan, which helped to personalize the idea and to associate it with its current sponsor.

The fight to get the money to pay the women guards was especially difficult. The author of the plan had been repeatedly critical of various actions of the City Council, and he was obviously not over-popular with the administration. One of the metropolitan papers actually suggested that the best way for Merriam to get his programs adopted would be for him to propose exactly the opposite (incidentally this was tried with some success several times). The original budget item was rejected by the Council. The second time around the circumstances were more auspicious, especially since the police commissioner himself was asking for some other adjustments in his budget. This time there was also more civic and newspaper support, and there had been additional pressure on the aldermen by mothers of school children. The proposal finally went through as à rider to another appropriation bill.

Timing and political compromise

No one can always say the right thing at the right time, but citizen-politicians need—perhaps more than people in most other activities—to develop some of the *savoir faire* that goes with a trigger-sensitive sense of timing.

Timing is tied in closely with another factor that can make or break planned political progress: the art of compromise. Nowhere else is the fine hand of the political master more noticeable or more needed. And nowhere does the citizen-politician need firmer grounding in conviction or more adaptability in execution. Political compromises are always tied in with personal integrity; they may also be tangled up with pride, face saving, or just stubbornness or ignorance. In politics, as elsewhere, it is important to be able to say generously and with sincerity "I was wrong. I begin to see that there is more to this than I thought. How about this alternative? It seems to me that it reconciles all our important differences. A least it is something we can all agree on. Let's start there and get going. I will withdraw my earlier objection." Finding the common denominator, even if one has to settle for less than one hoped, is firm starting ground. Indeed in a democracy it is the only possible place to start. When you can not convert the opposition, join them, at least as far as an alert but flexible conscience will permit.

Creative compromise is something more than horse-trading, though it will often result in trades. It is more than "I'll scratch your back if you'll scratch mine," though it may result in eased irritation on both sides. It is finding the all-important mutual ground and building a solid and prideful structure on it. It means taking the other fellow along with you, not simply beating him at his own game. This kind of compromise is the energizing factor of democracy; it is the force that makes

possible a new synthesis which in turn becomes a new foundation for still other constructive compromises. By definition
such compromises offer no threat to personal integrity; they
are rather the end-product of a creative imagination and the
will to cooperate. Most compromises made in the everyday
run-of-the-mill political wrangles fall short of this ideal. Most
of them are hastily precipitated to get something done *now*.
And it is not always easy to draw a line between the good and
the bad compromise, the honest and the dishonest trade. Often
the verdict depends on one's point of view. T. V. Smith in *The
Democratic Way of Life* [6] has spelled out many case histories
of the kinds of compromises which were his daily portion as a
state legislator. The statesmanlike politician, and citizen-politician, will want to hold high the torch of creative compromise as he inches forward in his handling of difficult civic
issues.

The process of making one's civic weight felt, therefore, is
many-faceted; politics has its rules, to be sure, but its substance and color escape tight definition. It is balance; tightrope
walking; the one-step-forward-and-the-half-step-back; the retreat in order to advance; the deployment around the opposition's blind quarter; the scouting expedition; the calculated
risk; the determined forward push that can fail ignominiously
or succeed gloriously. One thing is clear: *no mechanical
formula will process neatly measured units of political skills
so as to produce a foregone conclusion.*

The limits on the possible

Politics is an art—the art of the possible. It is an art because
it deals with unpredictable, fallible, though often wonderful,
people. It is an art because its success or failure depends on
delicate, moving adjustments operating within a framework
of limitations. These are often man-made and their nature,

[6] Rev. ed. (Chicago: University of Chicago Press, 1939).

form, substance, and significance merit the close scrutiny of every citizen, for it takes a trained eye and a sensitive touch to size up barriers to political action. A wall, forbidding as volcanic rock, can turn out to be as yielding as a sponge-rubber stage set; and what looks like a broad, fair high-way can suddenly be cut off as if by a clanging portcullis. And sometimes unseen barriers hide in a smothering fog, and one must inch one's way forward blindly. There are times when discretion is definitely the better part of valor. Even taking a tedious detour may be better than miring down in inaction.

No type of government can escape the limits on the possible; and the limits are sometimes set by the spareness of the human resources that can be devoted to the task at hand. Morale, skill, and vision all help to determine those limits. Even dictators have learned that citizen conviction is a more potent force than naked fear. They expend ingenuity, effort, and great sums of money in fostering contentment, or a reasonable facsimile thereof. They stretch the limits of the possible by means of devilishly skillful propaganda efficiently channeled. In the free world on the other hand the limits on the possible are, and must be, tied to honest persuasion, agreement, and consensus.

Politics, party politics, stands at the nexus of this process. The limits of what is politically possible *can be pushed out as citizens become productively involved in the political process,* for the character of citizen involvement writes every prescription of democratic government. Both political parties are constantly engaged in testing the limit of what is politically profitable. They have every incentive to stop well short of the impossible, for they are repeatedly taught the hard way to draw a line beyond which it does not pay to go. Yet, para-doxically, any party will wither away if it stands still too long. It must always keep moving into the future; substantial blocks of citizen support must somehow be harnessed to party goals, if they are to be attained. *Politics puts a premium on the art of making haste slowly—of pacing political goals.*

There is no more important or demanding political task than accurately to blend the productively conservative with the promising innovation. The effective citizen-politician not only needs deep understanding of people, institutions, and processes, he also needs ingenuity and perceptiveness. He needs the kind of weather-eye experience that produces the educated hunch; applied with artistry it will win political battles. Politics is truly a great game, one which every citizen can and indeed must play. No one ever really stands on the sidelines.

The call for citizen participation has never been more insistent than today, nor has it ever had a better chance of being answered. The life and death challenge of two world wars and the great depression have done much to cement a highly productive partnership between business, labor, agriculture, government, and citizens. Victories where they have been won—tentative though some of them are—have brought prestige to democratic institutions. If we have gained no more than a respite in a continuing struggle, at least we have seen the ideals of personal freedom and self-determination spread across the world.

Sobering years and heroic tasks have left a legacy of political education for all participants. These experiences which have been shared by millions of public servants and tens of millions of active citizen-politicians are leavening forces in the whole of public life. The nation is ripe for such leavening. It is rich and powerful, the leader of the Western axis in a world in ferment. It has become a living symbol of freedom; and its rising living standards are a beacon to billions of people still victimized by famines and deprivation. America has become a bulwark against the tyranny of communism. We have become a great power in an age where we cannot escape responsibility for brothers all around the world. Millions of

American soldiers, and hundreds of billions of American dollars have been poured into a worldwide struggle for the rights of man. It is true that much that we have done was accomplished because of narrow self-interest, but much of it also has welled up from deep democratic commitment to the rights of free men everywhere.

Such massive responsibilities have spawned global government operations and presented American democracy with severe tests. In every area governments have left behind them the leisurely personal give-and-take of the New England town meeting. We have to live within an increasingly complex web of government activities. We have more taxes to pay, more officials to elect, and more laws to obey. We have had to find ways and means of maintaining an awesome defense establishment, and our sons must serve their turn at the unfamiliar task of soldiering. Plain citizens have become both pawns and instruments in the war of ideologies, and their experiences cannot fail to contribute to our private political educations.

The integration of these personal experiences into meaningful democratic patterns is peculiarly the task of politics. The special-interest groups are likely to take myopic views of the total situation; the citizen-politician, as a citizen first and a partisan second, has a stake in larger issues. This stake is matched only by his responsibilities. He needs facts, he needs to know how to work through channels, and he needs leadership. In sum, he desperately needs strong, dedicated political parties.

Many of the tasks of politics require professionalism in the highest sense but often this professionalism can and must be exercised by volunteers. Politicians must become statesmen, and citizens must become politicians, and American democracy must plan to produce more of both.

But how can we expect men of dedication and distinction to assume the burdens of democratic government if we persist in treating politics with scorn? If we consider politicians as creatures of lesser breed? If we let our childern grow up thinking that "all politicians are crooks" and "politics is dirty"? How can we hope to keep the great complex of democratic government on even keel and plowing resolutely ahead unless we raise our children to be politicians?

It is of utmost importance to find ways of making the term "politician" an honorable one, even though this calls for a revolution in our private attitudes and in public morality. A many-faceted attack is necessary. Politicians and parties must be persuaded, driven, bludgeoned if necessary, into behaving in ways which can earn the respect and admiration of the public. But citizens too must learn to respect the demands of public service and of politics. In increasing numbers they must become citizen-politicians, mastering both the pleasures and the pains of political action. Only so will nonvoting disappear and government procedures as well as political parties be strengthened in their democratic uses.

The costs, personal as well as dollar, will be heavy. Good citizens must be willing to go into politics on a professional as well as an amateur status. Actually the two fields feed each other, for amateurs develop into professionals, and professionals retire to volunteer status. But once deeply involved in the game of politics no one is likely willingly to retire.

INDEX

absentee voting, 141, 143, 149
Adamowski, Benjamin, 27
AFL-CIO merger, 99
AFL political action committee, 94
American Farm Bureau Federation, 99
Americans for Democratic Action, 100, 161
American Heritage Foundation, 142
American Political Science Association, 107, 111
American Public Welfare Association, 156
American Society for Public Administration, 156
Australian ballot, 140

ballot box, 133–150
  see also Poll watching; Vote; Voting process
ballots, counting of, 142
  secret, 140
  short, 138
  types of, 140
Bauler, Paddy, 99
Berelson, B. R., 188 *n.*
Bethea, J. W., 197 *n.*
Blaine, James G., 195
Board of Education, attendance at open meetings of, 199
Board of Elections, 145, 147
bosses, "behind-the-scene," 104
boss rule, in cities, 169–170
brewing industry, influencing of legislature by, 177
bribery, 32
  in machine politics, 173
  public apathy toward, 178
bureaucratic strangulation, 158
Bureau of the Budget, 156

California State Brewers' Institute, 177
campaign, financing of, 38–40, 93–94, 124, 202–206
campaign buttons, 72
campaign contributions, 38–40, 93–94
campaign organization, formation of, 35–38
campaign strategy, Chicago mayoralty race, 40–49
campaign tactics, underhand, 33–34
candidate, assessment of, 134–139
  demands upon, during election campaign, 30–35
canvassing, house-to-house, 63, 73, 93
  by citizen-politician, 72

career jobs, limitations on, 154–155
  see also Civil service; Government jobs and service; Merit system
Case, Clifford, 195
caucuses, function of, 120–122
Cermak, Anton J., 11
chain-voting, 145–146
Chicago, Citizens-for-Merriam organization, 18, 22, 49, 161
  crime and politics in, 43
  Crime Committee, 15
  fraudulent registration in, 46–48
  ghost voting in, 145
  as "horrible example of city politics," 49
  mayoralty election, as example of civic attitudes and voting behavior, 187–193
  Municipal Tuberculosis Sanitarium, 12
  organized crime in, 12
  patronage system, 21, 24
  pre-election polls, 1954, 130–131
  school system reform, 12
  slum clearance, 12
  voting frauds, 40–41
  West Side bloc, 45
CIO Political Action Committee, 94, 100
citizen action, and two-party system, 74–108
citizen lobbyist, 203
citizen-politician, major contribution by, 72
  organization of, by political parties in government activity, 82
  vs. professional politician, 159–160
  responsibilities of, 122, 180, 210
  role of, in two-party system, 55, 108
citizen power, accumulation of, through voting, 194
citizen pressure, 197–201
Citizens For A Better Chicago, 16–17
Citizens-for-Merriam Organization, 18, 22, 49, 161
Citizens of Greater Chicago, 15, 102
Citizens Schools Committee, 102
citizenship, democratic responsibilities of, 54
city councils, attendance at open meetings of, 199
city manager system, 155
civic attitudes, as challenge to democracy, 186
  voting behavior and, 187–193
Civic Federation, 102

212

civic paralysis, dangers of, 186
civic participation, forms of, 190
 see also Citizen-politician
civilian employees, number of, in government, 157
civil service, extent of, 151–152
 salaries in, 165
Clark, Joseph, 99, 170
Cleveland, Grover, 195
close elections, case histories of, 195
coffee sips, in political campaign, 30, 36–37
Committee For A Better Chicago, 24
committeeman, local, 79
 national, 78
 state central, 79
communication, problem of, in political campaign, 129
communism, citizen-politician vs., 209
 vs. democracy, 2, 54
communist subversion, 61
Communists, political power of, 100, 102
Congress, control of, 91
 running for, 168–169
Congressmen, letters to, 198
convention, nomination of leaders by, 110–111
 "rigging" of, 119
convention system, vs. primary elections, 120
corruption, analysis of, 178–179
 machine politics and, 173
crime, politics and, 43

Daley, Richard, 27, 29, 120, 131
David, P. J., 111 *n.*
defamation, in political campaigns, 31–32
Del Sesto, Christopher, 141
democracy, citizen involvement in politics and, 208
 vs. collectivism, 2
 vs. communism, 54
 defined, 1
Democratic National Committee, 81
Democratic Party, factions in, 85
 and ideological frameworks, 83
Democratic-Republican Party, 89
Democratic Way of Life, The, 207
Democrats-for-Merriam Committee, 25
Denney, Reuel, 60 *n.*
Dewey, Thomas E., 131
 "election" of, 195
dictatorship, 95–96
 vs. two-party system, 75
disputed elections, 195
Dixiecrats, 95

donkey, as party symbol, 87
doorbell ringing, 37
 see also Canvassing, house-to-house
Douglas, Paul, 163

Eisenhower, Dwight D., 85, 91, 168
election laws, 147
election procedures, regulation of, 139–144
 voting frauds in, 144–147
 see also Ballot box; Ballots; Voting process
election results, tallying of, 142
elections, disputed, 195
 rigged, 145
 simplification of, 147–148
elective office, qualifications for, 167
elephant, as party symbol, 87
examinations, for government jobs, 155

Fair Deal, 83
Farmers' Union, 99
Federalist Party, 89
Federation of Tax Administrators, 156
Fetridge, Bill, 19
filibusters, 162
"fix," engineering of, 71
Fortune poll, 1948, 130
free elections, negligent attitude toward, 3
freedom, in democracy, 2
fundraising, as core of party activity, 92–95
 for political campaigns, 38–40
 see also Campaign contributions
fusion, as campaign strategy, 42, 120
 emphasis on and political hazards of, in Chicago mayoralty campaign, 24–29

Gallup, Dr. George, 54
Gallup poll, 1948, 130
gambling interests, 177
Garfield, James A., 151
"ghosts," in fraudulent registration, 46–48, 145
Glazer, Nathan, 60 *n.*
Goldman, R. M., 111 *n.*
Gosnell, Harold F., 124 *n.*, 187 *n.*
government, citizen participation in, 82
 complexity of, 157
 decentralized, 85
government employees, number of, 157
government jobs, examinations for, 155
 in machine politics, 174
 see also Civil service; Merit system
governmental responsibilities, requirements of, 157
Graham, Philip L., 94

Index

lton, Alexander, 89
riman, Averell, 195
arrison, Carter, 10
Hatch Acts, 80, 93, 158
Hayes-Tilden disputed election, 195
Hoover Commissions on Government Re-
    organization, 157
Hughes, Charles Evans, 195

independent candidates, write-in vote
    for, 114–117
independent parties, 100
independent vote, importance of, 90
independent voter, limited pressure of,
    136
    required signatures for, 114
Independent Voters of Illinois, 25, 63
Indiana ballot, 140
International City Managers' Associa-
    tion, 156

Jackson, Andrew, 89, 151
judicial appointments, 155
judicial favors, bribery and, 175–176

Keenan, Frank, 25, 49
Kennelly, Martin, 11–12, 25–27, 120
Kennon, Judge Robert, 196
"king-makers," in party nominating
    committees, 119
Knapp, Robert, 63, 68

Laborites, 100
labor organization, political power of,
    99–100
Labor's League for Political Education,
    100
labor racketeering, Senate probe of, 187
LaGuardia, Fiorello, 99, 170
lawyers, role of, in politics, 162
Lazarsfeld, P. F., 188 n.
leaders and issues, 109–132
League of Women Voters, 102, 137, 161
legislative bribery, 175
legislators, salaries of, 164–165
letter-writing campaigns, 197–198
Lewis, J. Hamilton, 10
licenses and franchises, sale of, 176
Lincoln, Abraham, 89
liquor interests, pressure from, 177
Literary Digest poll, 130
literature distribution of, 72
lobbyist, citizen, 203
    professional, 100, 102
Long, Huey, 196
Lubell, Sam, 188 n.

McCarthy, Joseph R., 95
machine politics, 171–173
McKibben, George, 20
McPhee, W. N., 188 n.
mailing lists, political, 56–57, 60
Massachusetts ballot, 140
merit system, 162
    criticism of, 153
    expansion of, 154
    vs. machine patronage, 175
    vs. spoils system, 152
Merriam, Charles E., 9, 124 n., 127 n.,
    187 n.
Merriam, Robert E., 9–49, 127 n., 142,
    197 n., 130–131
Merriam School Guard Plan, 205
Moore, Ed, 20
Moos, M., 111 n.
muckrakers, 176
Muir, David, 116
Municipal Finance Officers Association,
    156

Nast, Thomas, 197
national convention, selection of leaders
    in, 110–111
    see also Convention; Convention sys-
    tem
National Grange, 99
National Opinion Research Center, 130
National Republican Party, 89
National Research Council, 130
national-state-local government system,
    76
New Deal, 83
newspapers, political information sup-
    plied by, 136–137
new voters, registration of, 63
nominating petitions, for independent
    candidates, 115
nominations, democratic results in, 121
    machinery of, 109–122
    regulation of procedures for, 117
nonpartisan politics, 97–99
North Central Education Association of
    Chicago, 11

officeholders, public scrutiny of, 168
office seekers, qualifications for, 167
open hearings, attendance at, 199

parliamentary procedures, grounding in,
    161–162
partisanship, by-passing of, 97–98
party committeeman, selection of, 76–78
    see also Committeeman
party financing, see Campaign, financing
    of; Fundraising

party label, pulling power of, 86
party leaders, selection of, 109–122
party line, following of, 135
party loyalty, class distinctions and, 84
  dangers of, 108
  vs. ideological frameworks, 83
party machinery, 57
party meetings, attendance at, 59
party national committee, function of, 78
party organization, 76–81
  corruption in, 170
party platforms, 125–128
party, political, *see* Political party
party politics, citizen involvement in, and democratic government, 208
  history of, 169
  professionalism and, 151–181
party primary, *see* Primary elections
party professionals, training of, 160–163
party strategy, "detection" of, 60
party strength, measurement of, 89–92
party system, federated vs. integrated structure of, 80
patronage, 21, 151
  Chicago, 24
  in machine politics, 171, 174
  see also Spoils system
Pendergast, Tom, 98, 170
petitions, 197
  nomination by, 113–114
Phenix City, Alabama, corruption in, 186, 197
platform, *see* Party platform
policy lines, 85–86
policy makers, power of, 104
political action, as "art of the possible," 201–211
  citizen participation in, 185–211
political appointments, merit system and, 151–155
political attack, planning of, 202–206
political bosses, 104, 169–170
political change, slowness of, 201
political compromise, timing and, 206–207
political decisions, citizen's role in, 109–132
political gossip, 56–57
political groups, 99–101
political ignorance, vs. democracy, 3
political machine, defined, 171
  see also Machine politics
political parties, character and functions, 56–57, 74–76, 78–83, 96–106, 109–132, 134
  see also Party organization

political polls, public opinion and, 128–132
political power, foci of, 103–106
political schools, for party members, 161
politician, training of, 160–163
politics, as art, 207
  citizen's participation in, 55–56; *see also* Citizen-politician
  as honorable profession, 211
  nonpartisan, 97–99
  practical, beginner's guide to, 53–73
  professionalism and, 151–181
poll tax, 90
poll watching, 59, 72, 148–150
polls, public opinion, 128–132
posters, campaign, 72
"power of one," in close elections, 194–196
precinct, local, number of voters in, 61
precinct captain, duties and qualifications of, 63
precinct committeeman, aid from in joining party, 56
Precinct Manual for Citizens-for-Merriam, A, 63, 68
precinct worker, 59
  role of, 61–73
  see also Volunteer workers
precincts, political, number of in U.S., 61
President, letters to, 199
  salary and expense allowance of, 164–165
presidential elections, voting statistics on, 90
  disputed, 195
President's Committee on Administrative Management, 157
pressure groups, 99–103
"pressuring," process of, 104
primary elections, vs. convention system, 120
  open and closed, 111–113
  registration in, 56
primary legislation, tightening of, 112
priorities, establishment of by citizen-politician, 203
professionalism, political, advantages and importance of, 179–181
  and party politics, 151–181
  rising standards of, 156–158
professional organizations, 156
Prohibitionists, 100
propaganda, in molding of public opinion, 123
Public Administration Clearing House, 156

public employees, party fund solicitation of, 80–81
public office, headaches and rewards of, 163–166
public opinion, molding of by party, 122–124
   and political polls, 128–132
Public Personnel Association, 156
public policy, as motivating force, 83
   political activities and, 122–132
public works contracts, bribery and, 176

racial groups, political weight of, 100
racketeering, 177
rally, political, 42
Reed Thomas H. and Doris D., 160 *n.*
referendum, 138
registration, canvassing for, 63
   fraudulent, 46–48
   permanent, 145
   process of, 140
religious groups, political weight of, 100
Republican National Committee, patronage and, 175
Republican Party, defeat of in 1954 Chicago elections, 20
   and ideological frameworks, 83
   and moneyed interests, 84
Riesman, David, 60
Roberts, Dennis J., 141
Roosevelt, Franklin Delano, 11
Rosenbaum, George, 187 *n.*
running for office, qualifications for, 166–167

salutation, correct forms of, in political letters, 198
Samish, Arthur H., 177
Sampson, Milward, 195
Science Research Associates, 73
Senate Crime Committee, 177–178, 187
senatorial courtesy, 175
Shapiro, Lee, 187 *n.*, 191
Sheridan, Jay, 73
   precinct worker's experience described by, 65–70
"short pencil" technique, in fraudulent voting, 41, 146
single-party power, 95–96
slatemakers, exercise of power by, 118–119
slogans, as verbal symbolism, 87
slot machine operators, pressure from, 177
Smith, T. V., 207
Socialists, 100

Social Science Research Council, 130
special interests, 83, 101–102
split tickets, 147, 149
spoils system, 21, 151, 174–178
Steffens, Lincoln, 176
Stevenson, Adlai E., 81
Stierer, Robert, 187 *n.*

Taft, Robert A., 85
Tammany Hall, 170
television, in molding of public opinion, 123
television campaign, in Chicago mayoralty election, 23
third-party movements, U.S., 81
Thurmond, J. Strom, 85, 116
Tilden, Samuel, 195
Tories, 100
trade associations, political power of, 99
Truman, Harry S., 81, 131, 195
trust-busting, 176
Tweed, William Marcy, 197
two-party system, citizen action and, 74–108

unit rule, in party caucus, 121

volunteer workers, "generals" vs. "privates" in, 57, 58, 67–68, 70, 72, 161
   see also Precinct worker
vote, shut-in, 141
   single, cumulative power of, 194
   write-in, 114–117
vote-getting, on precinct level, 63–65
voters, disfranchising of, 142
   intimidation of, by machine, 173
   new, registration of, 63
voting, absentee, 141, 143, 149
   compulsory, 193
   see also Ballot box; Ballots
voting behavior, civic attitudes and, 187–191
   factors influencing, 192
voting frauds, 40–41, 144–147
voting machines, 142, 146
voting potential, 90–91
voting process, 139–148
voting record, American, 90

Warren, Chief Justice Earl, 99
Whigs, 100
Willkie, Wendell, 168
Wilson, Woodrow, 195
write-in campaigns, 117
write-in vote, 114–117

Young Democrats, 60
Young Republicans, 60